Dating Mr. Darcy
A Smart Girl's Guide to Sensible Romance

Inspired by Jane Austen's

Pride and Prejudice

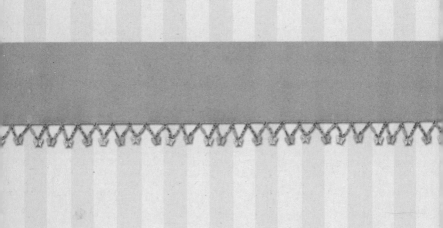

thirsty — Tyndale House Publishers, Inc., Wheaton, Illinois

Dating Mr. Darcy

A Smart Girl's Guide to Sensible Romance

Sarah Arthur

Visit Tyndale's thirsty Web site at areUthirsty.com

Visit www.saraharthur.com to learn more about Sarah Arthur.

Library of Congress Cataloging-in-Publication Data

Arthur, Sarah.
　Dating Mr. Darcy : a smart girl's guide to sensible romance inspired by Jane Austen's Pride and prejudice / Sarah Arthur.
　　p. cm.
　　ISBN-13: 978-1-4143-0132-7 (pbk.)
　　ISBN-10: 1-4143-0132-4 (pbk.)
　　1. Dating (Social customs)　2. Mate selection.　3. Man-woman relationships.　4. Single women—Psychology.　5. Austen, Jane, 1775-1817. Pride and prejudice.　I. Title: Dating Mister Darcy.　II. Title.
　　HQ801.A795 2005
　　646.7′7—dc22　　　　　　　　　　　　　　　　　　　2005002717

Printed in the United States of America

10　09　08　07　06　05
6　　5　　4　　3　　2　　1

For Chloe.

What's Inside

Note from the Author

Dear Reader,

I have a confession to make, happily married woman that I am:

I have a crush on Mr. Darcy.

Yep, I'm one of *those* Jane Austen fans. I firstP came to *Pride and Prejudice* through the BBC/A&E television series and haven't been quite the same person since. Gone are my ties to the Grunge Era, when we girls swooned for the slightly unshaven, plaid-wearing skaters playing hacky sack in the quad. Now, my husband is never more attractive to me than when

standing mildly aloof in his white button-down shirt
and prep-school tie, copping his smart-guy attitude.
He may roll his eyes at the world of Jane Austen, but
deep down he is my very own Mr. Darcy; and I am
Lizzy Bennet, laughing at him till he laughs at
himself. Having a crush on your husband is a good
thing.

But there were those dating years when I fell for
any number of unworthy guys, probably because I
hadn't yet encountered the ideal of Mr. Darcy by
which to judge them. Nor did I have a heroine like
Elizabeth Bennet to look up to. Sadly, I didn't read
Pride and Prejudice in high school when I should have,
when Lizzy would have been a welcome breath of
fresh air in the midst of daily relational disappoint-
ments. I don't know if the book just never crossed my
path or if I thought it was "Old English" or what.
And for whatever reason, Jane Austen was never
assigned reading material in my college literature
courses, either. It's a wonder I survived at all.

So when a friend loaned me the BBC/A&E
series several years ago during a particularly
wretched, flu-ridden February, I had no idea from

one scene to the next what was going to happen. Darcy's first proposal was a total surprise, as was Charlotte Lucas's marriage, Wickham's betrayal, and Lydia's elopement. I giggled at Mr. and Mrs. Bennet, hissed at Miss Bingley, and hollered, "You go, girl!" every time Lizzy said *anything*. Then when it was over, I watched it all again.

If only I had discovered Darcy during those dating years! And now that I've become immersed in all six of Jane Austen's major novels, I wish I'd read them long ago, over and over again, during those wasted hours in study hall. If you haven't read Austen either, take it from a literature buff with a romantic turn of mind: You're missing out.

Pride and Prejudice has never gone out of print since it was first published in 1813, making Jane Austen one of the most popular and beloved authors in the English language. Her popularity is not only because of her ironic wit and economical prose, but because of her timeless insights into human nature and romantic love. How an unmarried "spinster" could have had such tremendous insight into the nutty nuances of romantic relationships is a mystery and ongoing debate that perhaps will never be resolved. One could say that the closer we get to something, the more difficult it is to see it properly, which might account for why those of us who are "attached" sometimes can't seem to see our significant other or the relationship very clearly.

By the same token, you may be wondering what a married woman like myself might have to say to those of you who are still playing the dating game or despairing of ever finding your own Mr. Darcy. Good question. While I won't claim even remotely to have Jane Austen's powers of discernment, I'm happy to offer what insights I can, aided by my distance from the situation and my incurable addiction to romance.

If I'm hopelessly off base at times, I ask your forgiveness. As Elizabeth Bennet says, "We all love to instruct, though we can teach only what is not worth knowing." But if you, too, have a crush on Darcy, I hope you find yourself in good company!

I am very affectionately yours,
Sarah Arthur

Opening Thoughts

It is a truth universally acknowledged that a single girl in possession of her right mind must be in want of Mr. Darcy. Including you, we can assume, or you wouldn't have bothered to pick up this book. Whether you're single, dating, or otherwise, you're in good company, sister! Prepare yourself for an all-out Darcy Fest within these pages. (Careful, though: This is a spoiler, so you'd better know *Pride and Prejudice* from start to finish first.)

Clearly, we're not the only girls to fall in love with Mr. Darcy in the two hundred years since Jane

Austen immortalized his fine figure in her beloved novel. His romance with Elizabeth Bennet, given flesh and blood in recent films and spin-offs of *Pride and Prejudice*, has drafted thousands of admirers into the ranks of genuine Janeites and card-carrying Austenians. Keira Knightley proves that Jane Austen won't be going away anytime soon. And we can't forget the "a-Firthionados," who have become fervent fans over the years thanks to the eloquent eyes and wet shirt of Colin Firth. Mmm.

In fact, now that you mention it, the ten-year anniversary of the BBC/A&E television series obligates us to a celebratory marathon of all six episodes, don't you think? It's a tough job, but *somebody's* gotta do it. And for good measure, we might as well watch all the major films made of Austen's characters in the last decade: Gwyneth Paltrow and Jeremy Northam in *Emma*, for example; Kate Winslet, Emma Thompson, and Hugh Grant in *Sense and Sensibility*; and even teen queen Alicia Silverstone as a postmodern Emma in *Clueless*. Some Janeites have argued eloquently for *You've Got Mail* as yet another take on *Pride and Prejudice*. And why not?

Here we probably should give a nod to Bridget Jones, whose popularity can't be overstated but whose similarities to Elizabeth Bennet remain tenuous at best. As lovable as Bridget is to those of us who share her tendency to say all the wrong things at all the wrong times, we can't help thinking poor Mr. Darcy somehow ended up with Lydia at the conclusion of *that* story. (And, we suppose, if that Mr. Darcy chose such a match with his "eyes open," then he probably deserves her!)

> "In vain have I struggled. It will not do. My feelings will not be repressed. You must allow me to tell you how ardently I admire and love you."
> DARCY TO LIZZY

No, it's Jane Austen's own Mr. Darcy we return to time and time again. That's because our dear, darling Fitzwilliam embodies everything we romantics desire in the guy of our dreams: passion, integrity, honesty, intelligence, loving affection, and a willingness to accept us for who we really are, crazy family notwithstanding. Oh, and we can't forget the "something pleasing about the mouth" when he speaks. Hmm, yes. And how nice he looks in that formal dinner jacket . . .

Okay, so we're *hopeless* romantics when it comes to Darcy. We'll track him down in whatever form we can find him, all the while envisioning our own Mr. Darcy making his appearance in the ballroom of our lives. Whether we're dating or single, we have an ideal relationship in mind that looks something like our hero and Elizabeth Bennet gazing at each other across a crowded drawing room at Pemberley, eyes locked in mutual acknowledgment: *You were made for me.*

Sigh.

Yet for all his excellent exterior qualities, it's Darcy's inner character we admire most, or we'd be just as quick to snatch up books titled *Dating Mr. Wickham.* No, we want the good heart, not just the good looks. We want a guy with whom we can build the kind of romantic friendship that will outlast everything life throws our way.

Some of us are perhaps currently dating, which means we're assessing the Darcy Potential (DP) of our romantic attachments. This is a good thing. If we're not dating, we're perhaps despairing at the apparent lack of DP in the guys we know. Body piercings aside, how could any of them possibly live up to such a noble and—yes, let's be honest—*yummy* standard? One of the goals of this book is to help us assess the DP of the twenty-first-century guys in our lives, especially when it comes to their other relationships. More on that later.

Having said all that, as much as we swoon over Darcy, it's Elizabeth Bennet we really admire. Jane Austen herself once called her "as delightful a creature as ever appeared in print."[1] We want to be like Lizzy. We long to have the strength of character and depth of self-knowledge that allow us to turn down the offers and innuendos of an undeserving culture, that allow us to refuse even the dishy, the dashing, the delicious Mr. Darcys when they fail to grasp our true worth (at first, anyway). Because if we can be like Lizzy, we can overcome those lurking insecurities that make us question our own judgment in all matters relational and stop chasing empty dreams. Right?

Well, sort of. We easily lose sight of the key quality that makes Elizabeth Bennet so compelling:

She messes up.

Yep, even our dear Lizzy makes mistakes in judgment. In fact, the moment she recognizes her own willful prejudice against Darcy is when the entire story takes its ultimate romantic turn. That's when she finally faces what she's been ignoring. The rest is literary history.

At the risk of sounding like Mary Bennet, we must admit there's a lot to learn from the development of Lizzy's character. We can't help but be amazed at the acuteness of Jane Austen's discernment regarding the nuances of relationships, particularly in the arena of romance. Nothing escapes her eye. Every frailty of the human heart, every absurdity, is placed under a microscope for our inspection. Before we know it, we find our own motives and longings have been given the same kind of scrutiny. If we're honest with ourselves, we soon discover that we're prone to failure not only in judging our own hearts, but we often vastly misunderstand the people around us as well.

Eventually we come to realize that Jane Austen's remedy for our inherent lack of self-knowledge is to take time for reflection. We need to get alone and put some serious effort into honest self-evaluation. We must take ourselves to task for "what we have done" and "what we have left undone,"[2] as the old prayer of confession states. And this is the case not only in our romantic relationships, but in all our relationships: with family, with friends, and with God.

At some point or another, we all face the difficult task of looking inside ourselves. Do we have what it takes to live like Lizzy in the twenty-first century, in spite of our own loony family and friends? *Dating Mr. Darcy* is designed in part to help us consider our own EP, our Elizabeth Potential. It's a guide to the kind of sensible romance that Lizzy herself would approve of.

But in this quest we must not be impatient with ourselves, or with the possible (and impossible) Darcys in our lives. As Jane Austen lovingly wrote to her niece in 1817:

> "No—I cannot talk of books in a ball-room; my head is always full of something else."
> LIZZY TEASING DARCY

To you I shall say, as I have often said before, Do not be in a hurry, the right man will come at last; you will in the course of the next two or three years meet with somebody more generally unexceptionable than anyone you have yet known, who will love you as warmly as possible, and who will so completely attach you that you will feel you never really loved before.[3]

Sigh again.

Perhaps someday Jane's words of wisdom will be only too true in our own lives. Meanwhile, we have some important—and fun!—work to do.

How to Read This Book

Dating Mr. Darcy is meant to be an enjoyable romp through the land of romance, a romp in which we keep our heads on straight. We have much to learn from Elizabeth Bennet about the crucial importance of all our relationships and how they influence, for better or worse, our romantic attachments.

The first step is to become familiar with the story of *Pride and Prejudice*, whether in film or in print. If you're not already acquainted with Jane Austen's Mr. Darcy and Elizabeth Bennet, it's a good idea to be introduced before you read any further in *Dating*

Mr. Darcy. Once you've done so, the cast of characters listed at the back of this book can help you keep the main players straight. Locations are listed as well. You may also want to familiarize yourself with the story lines of *Emma* and *Sense and Sensibility*, as there will be occasional references to both.

If you're currently dating a potential Darcy, this book is for you. This is your opportunity to take a step away from the relationship and consider how both you and your significant other are doing in the grand scheme of things. Are you personally maintaining a healthy sense of your own identity, particularly when it comes to your family, friends, and faith? And how about Darcy: Do you have a clear understanding of who this guy really is when it comes to *his* family, friends, and faith?

Or perhaps you're still looking for your Mr. Darcy, in which case this book is also for you. Now is the time—while you're waiting for him to either show up or declare himself—to take a thorough, honest assessment of all your relationships. All of Jane Austen's heroines reflect on what they know about themselves, which in turn helps them assess their romantic interests. For just a bit, take your mind off assessing (and obsessing about) the DP of the guys you know and concentrate on your own character instead. What's your EP?

For those of you who hope you've found your Mr. Darcy and are ready to think long-term, now is a good time to assess the PP, or Pemberley Potential, of your relationship. As a couple, how healthy are your interactions with each other's families, friends, and faith? What sort of Pemberley are you creating: Is the relationship a blessing or a burden to others?

To aid in these reflections, *Dating Mr. Darcy* is divided into several parts. Part one explores the "dating market" today as compared to Jane Austen's time. It also highlights the timeless wisdom we can glean from the example of Elizabeth Bennet in terms of how to conduct ourselves in the crazy arena of twenty-first-century romance. In parts two, three, and four, we take a look at why family, friends, and faith matter in dating relationships. With Lizzy and Darcy as test subjects, we'll assess how healthy your relationships are in all of those areas. In part five, we'll explore the necessity of taking time for honest reflection to come to a better understanding of ourselves and others.

The final section of this book contains two resources to help you in the process of figuring out what is going on with you and your various relationships. First there's a Guide to Reflection with ideas for a personal miniretreat to help you listen to what God and your heart are telling you. The second resource is affectionately entitled "Lizzy Bennet's Diary," the newly discovered, original, uncut version. Yep, you won't find this anywhere else. That's because, as the lovable and flawed heroine of your own story, you get to write it! There are diary entries to help you assess all your relationships and Darcy's too, complete with quiz questions, quips, and quotes.

So let's go to it!

Part One

Pressure and Promiscuity

- Why Jane Austen can give us tips for the Dating Game
- Installing your Creep Detection System
- How to avoid the Love Nest Syndrome

Part One

PRESSURE AND PROMISCUITY

Our ball was rather more amusing than I expected. . . . The melancholy part was, to see so many dozen young women standing by without partners, and each of them with two ugly naked shoulders!

JANE AUSTEN IN A LETTER TO HER SISTER, CASSANDRA, DECEMBER 9, 1808[4]

The next time you're really bored on a Friday night, flip through the cable channels or the pages of a recent girl mag and count the belly buttons, bare legs, and cleavage. Seriously. Keep track on a piece of scrap paper: fifteen innies, twelve outies, thirty-six bare legs, eighteen thighs, twenty-four bosoms, etc.

Any bare backs, bikini tops, or naked torsos with certain areas coyly covered? Add those too. Then divide the total by four and treat yourself to the same number of large scoops of caramel-latte-macadamia-nut-chunk ice cream. Go ahead: make yourself sick.

Despite the retro-preppie fashion movement, a quick survey of today's magazines, TV episodes, movies, and Super Bowl halftime shows proves that girls are exposing more skin than ever. What's *that* about? If we are supposedly so "liberated" compared to, say, when Jane Austen published *Pride and Prejudice* in 1813, why are we still tempted to offer our physical bodies as our greatest and only attribute?

Welcome to the Relationship Market, otherwise known by the more humane title of the Dating Game (though "game" still implies winners and losers). It's the public auction where single girls and guys advertise their (mostly physical) attributes in order to get the attention of the opposite sex.

> "I do not particularly like your way of getting husbands."
> LIZZY TO LYDIA

Okay, so that's putting it rather bluntly. But you know exactly what's going on. And so did Jane Austen, our beloved authoress.

In fact, the pursuit of romantic attachments in the twenty-first century is eerily similar to what young people went through in Jane Austen's time. Singles in the dating "market" often have only brief, contrived opportunities to get to know each other and decide whether or not a person's character or personality fits theirs. Much like the young people of Regency England, we often congregate at "watering places" where other singles are likely to be and parade our best attributes in order to gain the attention of a potential partner.

And, as in Jane Austen's time, those of us who are respectable still dance the intricate dance of healthy relationships while the silly and selfish pursue paths that lead to pain for themselves and others. We girls may feel like we have more power than ever to choose for ourselves which guy to date or marry (or not), but to a large extent culture still dictates how to

look, what to wear, what to say, and how to "advertise" ourselves to the opposite sex.

Yes, as much as it disturbs us, the metaphor of
the "market" in reference to relationships is, unhap-
pily, still current. This doesn't mean we like it. That
any of us would put ourselves up for sale in *any*
century is degrading to our sense of human dignity.
To our disgust and annoyance, guys still respond to
the female form, and girls still respond to guys'
responses to the female form. And round and round
it goes.

> ⊗ ⊗ ⊗
> "Adieu to
> disappointment and
> spleen. What are men
> to rocks and
> mountains?"
>
> LIZZY, ON BEING
> INVITED TO TRAVEL
> WITH HER AUNT AND
> UNCLE TO THE
> LAKE DISTRICT

Perhaps that's why we girls are
intuitively drawn to Jane Austen.
The world's most famous writer of
romantic comedy wrestled firsthand
with the realities of the relationship
market, though the stakes were argu-
ably much higher back then (i.e.,
we're not likely to end up destitute
in spinsterhood, dependent on the financial assistance of our older brothers).

While she was a young woman in her early twenties, Jane Austen met and flirted with a cute young Irishman by the name of Tom Lefroy, who, historians suspect, might have married her if she'd had any money (creep). Later Jane accepted a marriage proposal from a family friend, but then turned him down the next morning. Some biographers suggest that she refused yet another offer later on. By that time she was a novelist. We get the sense from her letters that her identity now rested in her *ability*, not her *marketability*. How many of us would have the self-awareness to do the same?

In the same way that we're intrigued by Jane Austen, we're also drawn to the character of Elizabeth Bennet. Like Lizzy, we don't want to play the "market" in any of its forms. We don't want to put our "wares" on display for the admiration of the Mr. Collinses or Mr. Wickhams in order to feel secure about our own body image, if not our future. We don't want to gear all our words and actions toward pleasing, intriguing, or enchanting every eligible bachelor who comes our way. Not only is the prospect exhausting, but it grates on our sense of dignity and self-respect. If guys can't deal with us as we are, then it can't be worth bothering about them, right?

Yeah! So there!

The problem is, we're wired by God to be in loving relationships with the opposite sex, which hopefully isn't a problem *after* we find those relationships. In the meantime, we long to be special in someone's eyes: to capture his attentions, win his affections, and make him feel lonely when we're not around. When an attractive single male enters the room, we pick up a signal somewhere in our relational radar that activates our marketing instincts, try as we might to override them. A sudden urge to smooth our hair, pick the lint off our skirt, and rub the lip gloss off our teeth takes us by force, and we find ourselves prisoner to our deepest insecurities. We *know* we shouldn't care that this Bingley or Darcy or whoever he is has just entered our field of vision. But we *really* wish we'd worn a different skirt.

Lizzy herself is only too human in this regard. While in agony as to whether or not Darcy still cared for her, "she followed him with her eyes, envied every one to whom he spoke, had scarcely patience enough to help anybody to coffee; and then was enraged against herself for being so silly!"

Phew. So we're not the only ones.

But Lizzy needn't worry. What Darcy has grown to appreciate most are her inner qualities, not the color of the dress she's wearing, though his initial reaction to her outward appearance at the Meryton Assembly is one of bored indifference. Silly boy! It takes Lizzy's lengthy visit to Netherfield during Jane's illness for him to begin to admit that not only is Elizabeth Bennet attractive in her own right, but she holds an unexpected fascination for him, largely because she isn't conscious of her looks and refuses to play games. (Of course, when compared to the sly tactics of Miss Bingley or the wild flirtations of Lydia, any girl looks modest.)

This doesn't mean Lizzy is meek and unassuming, however. Once she gets past her initial intimidation, she engages Darcy in verbal sparring that has the unintentional consequence of making him fall head over heels in love with her. "Now be sincere," she teases him after they get engaged; "did you admire me for my impertinence?" And he replies, "For the liveliness of your mind, I did." Mmm. A guy who falls for us because of our wit and intelligence? Yum.

Yet when this unconscious bewitchment first begins, Darcy is alarmed. He quickly reverts back to assessing Elizabeth Bennet's outward traits in order to keep himself "safe" from her intriguing inner qualities. As Austen writes, "Darcy had never been so bewitched by any woman as he was by her. He really believed, that were it not for the inferiority of her connections, he should be in some danger." In other words, he thinks to himself, *Okay, so she's smart. And pretty. But what about her* obnoxious *family and friends? Dude, don't go there.*

At first this strikes us as extremely snobby, and

of course it is. But part of what's going on is Darcy's acknowledgment that our family and friends play a large role in who we really are. In fact, our connections form a major part of our identity and eventually influence our romantic attachments, whether we like it or not. Our connections become his connections too, even when we're just dating. Darcy understands this principle to some extent, though he makes the mistake of seeing Lizzy's family and friends themselves as points against her rather than looking at her character in light of those relations. Had he inspected further, he would have seen a girl doing her best to be a wise and patient daughter, a caring sister, a faithful friend, and a respected young woman in the community.

He also would have seen a girl of faith and moral conviction, someone who acknowledges there is a higher rule or law that guides our speech and actions in all of our relationships. This moral law says we are responsible for the pain others experience as a result of our selfish words and actions. We will deal with the consequences someday, if not in this lifetime then certainly when we stand face-to-face with God. We are accountable to God for the way our romantic relationships might hurt those who love us best—something Lydia, for example, fails to grasp and Wickham chooses to ignore.

But Darcy at first decides not to probe too deeply into Lizzy's character as a daughter, sister, friend, and person of faith. He prefers to keep his distance. And Lizzy treats him with the same dismissive attitude. Judging a guy's character without taking into account his family background, the quality of his friendships, and the strength of his moral convictions is a dangerous business.

Very dangerous. When it comes to guys like Wickham, a girl's got to have her Creep Detection System fully functioning. Unfortunately, Lizzy is just as blinded at first by Wickham's outward appearance of goodness as she is by Darcy's outward appearance of smug arrogance. Because Wickham is cute and friendly, she easily falls for his half-truths and outright lies about Mr. Darcy. Even when Lizzy's sister Jane questions how Darcy could get away with such awful behavior, Lizzy insists that Wickham couldn't have made up the story. "Besides," she says, "there was truth in his looks."

Eek! Lizzy is the *last* person we'd expect to win the prize for Most Gullible. If *she* falls for the resident hunk, what does that mean for the rest of us?

We're toast, that's what it means. All of us will get burned at some point or another. That's because we're created to find certain facial features, mannerisms, and body types attractive, and we often find ourselves attracted to a guy on the basis of those characteristics before our brain has time to kick in. This isn't necessarily a bad thing every time. As you've no doubt been told a million times, physical attraction is a God-given gift that all healthy couples enjoy. You don't want to make a commitment to someone you have no attraction for, or your disinterest could quickly turn to repulsion (think *Charlotte Lucas*). But you also don't want to make an emotional attachment to a guy on the basis of his stunning profile alone. Or the way he looks in that button-down Oxford. Or the cute little dimple in his chin. Or the . . .

Right. Get ahold of yourself. This is where the sensible side of you is supposed to kick in.

As Lizzy discovers after reading Darcy's letter of explanation, it's far too easy to let your emotions lead you off track in your assessment of someone. "Pleased with the preference of one," she chastises herself, "and offended by the neglect of the other, on the very beginning of our acquaintance, I have courted prepossession and ignorance, and driven reason away, where either were concerned." She reviews the attributes of Wickham's character and realizes she's been deceived, while Darcy has in fact been the best sort of guy all along: an esteemed friend, an affectionate brother, and someone with strong moral values. Eventually she comes to realize that he's exactly the sort of guy with whom she could make a serious commitment for life.

"Whoa," you're saying right about now. "Who said anything about serious commitment? I just want to have fun here. Give me Wickham any day rather than a boring weekend at home babysitting my little brother." Point well taken. Marriage may be a long way off, and there's plenty of time to play the Dating Game for a while before getting really serious. . . . And yet, like Lydia Bennet, perhaps we *should* take everything a bit more seriously after all. Not because we're going to be married by the time senior prom or even grad school rolls around, but because all the habits we form in our dating relationships become the (often shaky) foundation on which our marriages are built down the road. Yep, it's never too soon to consider whether those habits are good or bad, healthy or unhealthy, just as we need to pay attention to the food we eat and the grades we get in school. Everything we do now has consequences later, and that's true in romance too.

> "Women fancy admiration means more than it does."
> "And men take care that they should."
> JANE AND LIZZY

So let's say Mr. Darcy has entered the ballroom of your life, whether as a date or a prospect. As Lizzy can tell you, beware the "Love Nest Syndrome," where no one except your Number One Crush is invited to be part of your life anymore. That's exactly what Darcy himself wants to create with Lizzy in his first marriage proposal. He tells her, in so many words, "I want you so badly, I'm determined to ignore my family, my friends, and my moral principles in order to have you."

Now, for a fleeting moment that sounds horribly romantic: "He's going to throw all that away for *me*? Because he loves *me*?" But Elizabeth is sensible enough to see the audacity of his words. She recognizes instantly that it's impossible to ignore those other factors when it comes to romance. We simply can't pretend our family, friends, and faith don't exist. They are at the core of who we are.

It's far too easy to think of dating Mr. Darcy as this bubble that protects and secludes you from all other relationships. Sure, your family and friends are important, but sometimes you'd like to change your name and zip code and start over. The truth is, as Jane Austen so eloquently expressed, those rela-tionships—as well as your faith commitments—are ground zero for your romantic attachments. This is the arena in which your character is tested, tried, perfected, and strengthened.

So the question of gauging a guy's DP is bigger than simply figuring out his favorite Slurpee flavor or ideal movie. It's more than merely assessing what you think you know about his virtues and vices. What reality TV fails to show is that a guy's character is primarily shaped by his other relationships, and if you're clueless about who this guy is in the context of his family, friends, and faith, you're clueless about who he is, period.

Not only that, but you need to consider how well you know *yourself* in all of those areas too. Forget

> "I might as well enquire," replied she, "why with so evident a design of offending and insulting me, you chose to tell me that you liked me against your will, against your reason, and even against your character?"
>
> LIZZY TO DARCY, AFTER REJECTING HIS FIRST PROPOSAL OF MARRIAGE

how that skirt looks on you for a moment: How well
are you getting along with your dad or stepmom
lately? When was the last time you honestly reviewed
your faults and set goals for improvement? If Lizzy is
any indication, you are strongest when you know
yourself on the inside, not just the outside. That's
the most crucial way to gauge your own EP.

And take it even one step further: How well
does *Darcy* know you in those areas? Has he spent
one-on-one time with your brother lately? Do you
let your friends hang out with the two of you? Do you
ever discuss church together? Because who you are in
those settings is the best indicator of how you'll
develop and mature as a woman who will love him as
a partner and friend.

In fact, the only way your relationship with Mr.
Darcy will be as healthy and wonderful as it can be is
if all your other relationships are healthy too—or at
least as healthy as you can try to make them.

So let's start by looking at family.

Had Elizabeth's opinion been all drawn from her own family,
she could not have formed a very pleasing picture
of conjugal felicity or domestic comfort.

Pride and Prejudice, VOLUME TWO, CHAPTER NINETEEN

So you're on your first date with a guy, and the
subject of family comes up, oh so casually. With the
firm resolve of Elizabeth Bennet, you decide to be
absolutely up-front and honest with him: After all,
there's no use hiding what will become painfully
obvious the minute he meets any of them. Even so,

you find yourself describing your nutty relations in as light a tone as possible, using words like "unique" and "animated." But you can tell his radar is probing beneath the surface. He's reading between the lines. Soon you notice beads of sweat on his forehead. And then comes the deer-in-the-headlights look. Not many minutes later, he glances at his watch and mutters something about the parking meter. End of story.

Well, hopefully not. But there's no denying it: Your family is often the litmus test for whether or not a dating relationship will succeed for the long-term, even into marriage. Yes, God has established marriage as a community of two in which a guy and girl leave their fathers and mothers and create a new family (Genesis 2:24). However, this doesn't mean you say good-bye forever to the homestead. Too often it's tempting to prematurely make the break from family when you're still only dating (back to the Love Nest Syndrome again!), forgetting or ignoring the fact that until you get married and leave

the home circle, your relatives are your most important relationships. Family shapes who you are.

This is also true for your Mr. Darcy. Darling
Fitzwilliam is the direct product of whatever
Pemberley he grew up in. His habits, mannerisms,
attitudes, values, beliefs, memories, ways of communicating, likes and dislikes—in short, all the important things about him—are shaped by the countless
hours he has spent with key family members throughout his life. We might call this his
"culture," or the patterns of behavior that signal how his family is
unique from others. While he may
be dissimilar in many ways to his
relatives, his behavior is nonetheless
a direct response to their culture.

> "Will you allow me,
> or do I ask too much,
> to introduce my sister
> to your acquaintance
> during your stay
> at Lambton?"
> DARCY TO LIZZY

You, too, were raised with certain values,
beliefs, attitudes, traditions—even quirky ways of
saying words or phrases—that identify you as a Lucas
or a Bingley or a Bennet or a Whatever. As much as
you might like to put Longbourn behind you forever,

it's still your home culture; and your character is best understood in that context. This doesn't mean you must be "always at Longbourn" (as Darcy so cryptically says to Lizzy) in terms of how influential your family continues to be in your adult life. But it does mean that you occasionally assess your behavior and acknowledge those moments when your Bennet-ness takes over.

Perhaps that's why getting to know a potential Darcy and his family sometimes feels like a diplomatic mission to a foreign country. Or like getting stuck in an *Alias* rerun. Gathering extensive files of eccentric details might be a good plan. *(Note to self: Darcy's cousin inquires as to health, etc., before giving hug. Perhaps is pathophobe? Thinks I might be deathly ill and contagious?)* Understanding Darcy means spying out things like, What are his happiest and saddest memories? What's his general attitude toward male authority figures? How does he treat the women in his family? How much does he embrace the rules, values, and structure of his home? The composite picture you get after collecting all those details will be more authentic to who Darcy really is than if you fail to launch the investigation at all.

Such thorough detective work pays off in the long run. For example, you might think that the guy who is willing to blow off family responsibilities on the weekends in order to spend time with you is simply proving his maturity and independence, not to mention how much he digs you. But if you follow the logical progression of the relationship from its beginnings to its desired outcome, it suddenly hits you that you'll eventually be his *wife*, which means you'll be a member of his family. And if you've observed that he repeatedly treats family with a lack of respect and attention, then what's to stop him from treating you in the same way in the long run? (And the correct answer is NOT "The fact that I'm so adorable.")

It's the kind of detective work Lizzy should do when meeting Wickham for the first time. His mannerisms are so charming that she easily assumes his good looks reflect a good heart. And *he* is sharp enough to realize she's the kind of girl who probably values family. So he shares a host of half-truths about his past as a "family man," focusing on his relationships with his father and with the father figure of the elder Mr. Darcy. Sure enough, Lizzy falls for it. She takes what he says about himself at face value and fails to confirm his words with those who knew him previously. She also fails to balance what he says with what he does. Only later does she try to "recollect some instance of goodness, some distinguished trait of integrity or benevolence" in his character, but she can't think of any. When he finally runs off with Lydia, Lizzy holds no hope that he will suddenly become a committed family guy after his behavior so far. And neither do we.

Flash forward two hundred years, and it's clear things haven't changed much when it comes to the influence of family on our lives.

> ● ● ●
> Brother in law of Wickham! Every kind of pride must revolt from the connection.
>
> LIZZY, MAKING ASSUMPTIONS ABOUT DARCY'S ATTITUDE TOWARD HER NOW THAT WICKHAM AND LYDIA ARE MARRIED

One of the unforgettable things about Jane Austen's novels is the crazy domestic situations she's able to create. Perhaps she had plenty of real-life material to work from. We look at characters like Lizzy and Lydia and wonder how they could come from the same parents. We find it hilarious, not only from a narrative standpoint, but because we've seen the same thing in real life even today. The Simpson sisters, anyone?

As for her own family, Jane's biographers tell us she was the younger of only two girls in a bevy of brothers. Like Elizabeth and Jane Bennet (and Elinor and Marianne Dashwood in *Sense and Sensibility*), Jane and her sister, Cassandra, were very close all of their lives, and though Cassandra was once engaged to a young man who died abroad, the sisters never married and lived together with various members of their family until Jane's death.

Jane herself wasn't necessarily the perfect relative. Her letters reveal her to be occasionally crabby, sarcastic, and uncharitable. (Who isn't?) While she was

remembered by her nieces and nephews as a loving
and cheerful aunt overall, some biographers suggest
that she may have struggled to keep a good attitude
about caring for her mother, for example, especially
after her father died. But as one historian writes,
"[Jane's] love for her family, tiresome though she
found some of its members to be, was unswerving."[5]

Because of Jane Austen's focus on the home, it's
not hard to see why family is the
axis around which Lizzy and Darcy's
relationship turns in *Pride and Prejudice*. At first, their families are what
keep them apart. He can't stand
hers and says so in such an obnoxious way in his first proposal that
Lizzy is furious. But his words make
their mark, and Lizzy is mortified to realize just how
much her family's behavior affects her and Jane's
opportunities for creating and keeping meaningful
romantic attachments. How many of us can relate!

Yet Lizzy is not willing to give up her family in

> "Could you expect me
> to rejoice in the
> inferiority of your
> connections? To
> congratulate myself on
> the hope of relations,
> whose condition in life
> is so decidedly
> beneath my own?"
>
> DARCY TO LIZZY, AFTER
> SHE'S REJECTED HIS FIRST
> MARRIAGE PROPOSAL

order to make the great escape Darcy offers in his first marriage proposal. That's because she recognizes what so many of us, including Lydia, fail to understand: that is, whether or not we like it, we're accountable to our parents and even our siblings for what happens in our romantic relationships. And as we've already said, the healthier our relationships are with family, the stronger and healthier our relationships with the opposite sex will be.

So how do we measure the health of our family dynamics, not to mention the health of our Darcy's familial relationships? Well, besides scheduling appointments with a professional therapist (not a bad idea), we can pay attention to three key areas: (1) respect, (2) communication, and (3) integrity. While the Bennets are a good example of what *not* to do in most of those areas, the Darcys don't necessarily win any gold stars either, especially if you factor in Lady Catherine de Bourgh. But both Lizzy and Darcy are decent models for giving it our best shot.

Respect

WHAT WASHING THE DISHES HAS TO DO WITH YOUR LOVE LIFE

"An unhappy alternative is before you, Elizabeth. From this day you must be a stranger to one of your parents.—Your mother will never see you again if you do not marry Mr. Collins, and I will never see you again if you do."

MR. BENNET, VOLUME ONE, CHAPTER TWENTY

Is your mom having another premenopausal melt-down because you forgot to get your stuff out of her car again? Take your cue from Lizzy: Mom still deserves your respect. And we're not talking just a cute little Regency curtsy, either; we're talking about a heartfelt "I'm sorry" and a genuine attempt to look at things from your mom's perspective next time. The more you get in the habit of taking an unselfish view of things around the home, the healthier your behavior will be toward your very own Mr. Darcy down the road.

Every human being is created in the image of God (see Genesis 1:27), which means every person deserves your respect, starting with your family. To disrespect the members of your family is to disrespect the Creator who took such care in forming each individual into a complex work of art. On top of that is the mandate to honor your parents (see Deuteronomy 5:16). Add a few siblings into the mix, and you could easily spend all evening at the dinner table saying, "*You* first. No, *you*." Oh, for the natural sweetness of Jane Bennet!

To respect someone means to treat their ideas, personal space, belongings, and needs as equal in importance to your own, while to honor someone means to treat all those things as *more* important than your own. The Bible says, "Be humble, thinking of others as better than yourselves" (Philippians 2:3). And the biblical call to respect doesn't depend on whether the other person deserves it, either.

Even though Lizzy finds her parents' behavior frustrating—not to mention extremely embarrassing at times, especially when Darcy is around—she treats them with a level of respect that is proactive rather than reactive. Instead of thinking, *Okay, I'm only going to be nice to Mom today if she's in a good mood*, she chooses ahead of time to be nice to Mrs. Bennet and not react to whatever the woman's attitude happens to be. She also doesn't join her father in making jokes at her mother's expense, though she's probably sorely tempted at times. Honoring her parents is a priority for Lizzy, even when they've failed to honor each other.

She also chooses to obey them, a concept we twenty-first-century girls sometimes have a hard time grasping. When Mrs. Bennet suspects that Lizzy will try to escape from Mr. Collins's marriage proposal, she says, "Lizzy, I *insist* upon your staying and hearing Mr. Collins." Austen writes, "Elizabeth would not oppose such an injunction." In other words, Lizzy understands the biblical mandate for children to obey their parents since "this is the right thing to do" (Ephesians 6:1). She will stay and hear Mr. Collins because her mother has asked her to.

This doesn't stop Lizzy from speaking the truth

when it involves her future well-being, however. She refuses to let her mother's poor judgment be the means of ruining her life. Lizzy will *not* marry Mr. Collins. And thankfully her father supports her decision, though it creates yet another rift with Mrs. Bennet for both father and daughter.

We all struggle to balance honoring our parents with establishing healthy boundaries between them and us. Yes, your mom has the right to ask you to clean the bathroom or give her a ride to the airport. And you have the duty to honor her reasonable requests. But she does not have the right to make you choose between her and your dad, for example, or to belittle you in front of your friends. By the same token, you have no right to blow up at her when you're having a bad day, just because she's your mom and supposedly she can handle it. Respectful boundaries go both ways.

"My child, let me not have the grief of seeing you unable to respect your partner in life. You know not what you are about."

MR. BENNET TO LIZZY, UPON LEARNING OF HER ENGAGEMENT TO MR. DARCY

Still, some of us long to have caring, unselfish moms and dads like Lizzy's aunt and uncle Gardiner, and many of us do, though we often fail to realize how blessed we are. Yes, Mr. and Mrs. Bennet are present in their daughters' lives, but more often than not, Lizzy and Jane end up acting as the mature and wise adults in the household—parenting their parents, you might say. And some of us have found ourselves in that same position. We look around us and feel like yelling, "Is there a grown-up in the house? Is anyone thinking about anyone else around here, or am I the only one who isn't being selfish?"

You're not alone, sister. A lot of us today some-how end up parenting our parents, and this is true for many of the guys we meet too. It's hard to respect adults who can't govern themselves. That's why guys sometimes struggle to respect *us* if they've had no good model for how mature men are supposed to treat women; and that's why we sometimes fail to respect *them*, because we can't picture any other way of interacting with guys than the example our mothers have shown us.

So where do we get good examples of respect between the sexes? Lizzy and Jane, at least, have the model of their aunt and uncle Gardiner to turn to. The Bennet sisters know what a healthy marriage looks like because the Gardiners demonstrate mutual love and respect. Like Lizzy and Jane, many of us resort to forging strong family ties outside the home circle because we're hungry for mentors. If we've lost a dad or mom through divorce, absence, abandonment, or even death, it's crucial that we find other people we can look up to.

Which brings us to our daunting, distinguished, delectable Mr. Darcy. (You *knew* we couldn't neglect him for long!)

Fitzwilliam's parents have already died, so he's the acting parent of the household for his younger sister, Georgiana. In fact, his close relationship with Miss Darcy alerts Lizzy to the fact that, at least within his own domestic circle, Mr. Darcy is a kind and loving guy—the furthest thing from proud. Even Wickham is forced to admit that Darcy is a good brother whom Georgiana highly respects as a parent figure. Through Darcy's relationship with his sister, Lizzy begins to see him in such an entirely new light that she begins to fall in love with him in spite of herself.

> [Darcy's] wish of introducing his sister to her, was a compliment of the highest kind.
>
> FROM *PRIDE AND PREJUDICE*

Respect for family is an important thing to pay attention to in any guy's character: How does he treat his nearest relatives, particularly his parents and the women in his life? In Darcy's case, though his dad is no longer alive, Darcy clearly loved and honored him and did his best to follow his wishes. And though his mom isn't alive either, Darcy is highly respected by the female members of his household, including the housekeeper. Finally, despite the fact that his aunt Lady Catherine de Bourgh is just as difficult to deal with as Mrs. Bennet, if not more so, Darcy does his best to be polite. Well, until she insults his Lizzy and threatens his own happiness, that is! But eventually Lizzy persuades him that his aunt should be extended the courtesy of an invitation to Pemberley.

Ah, yes. Courtesy. It's an aspect of respect that has long-term ramifications for our romantic relationships. Our parents have to teach us how to say please and thank you when we're little because politeness isn't something that comes naturally to us. What does come naturally is the impulse to have what we want and do what we want *now*, regardless of anyone else. British society in Jane Austen's day tried to get those impulses under control through cordiality, and perhaps those folks were onto something. Politeness forces us to consider how our words might affect the listeners. As Proverbs 15:1 says, "A gentle answer deflects anger, but harsh words make tempers flare." Courtesy defuses potential conflict.

And yes, courtesy applies to your annoying little sister, too. Let's say you have a Lydia in your life who thinks nothing of commandeering items in your wardrobe or flirting with your boyfriend on the phone. Do you play the game by her rules, like Kitty, and rudely snatch your jeans out of her grasping claws? Or do you employ Jane Bennet's endless patience? Between Jane and Kitty, it's easy to see who is better equipped for a peaceful romance down the road.

If you still live at home with one or more siblings, chances are the Osbournes aren't a bad comparison at times. On the other hand, you may be one of those lucky few whose sister or brother is more like a best friend, an ally against the hostile environment of school or the wacky atmosphere of home. Like Lizzy and Jane or Darcy and Georgiana, you've become close because you've known each other longest, share many of the same memories, and speak the same language. Even though your personalities might be different, you've learned to trust one another as friends for life.

So sisters are one thing. How do you treat your brothers, if you have any? You may think this has nothing to do with dating, but don't be too sure. It's far too easy to bring all the habits you develop with your brothers into your dating relationship, especially since your brothers are probably similar in age to your boyfriend. Take for example those moments when your date sounds off in the same tone as your brother, and out of habit you drop a condescending Big Sister remark that deflates his ego in an instant. Is that what he has to look forward to for the rest of his life? On the positive side, treating your brother with respect and courtesy gets you in the habit of treating your Mr. Darcy that way too.

When it comes to respect, actions often speak louder than words. This includes the little daily courtesies of life, particularly in the common areas of your home, such as the bathroom and the kitchen. If you're not doing your own dishes when you place them in the sink, who is? Practice thinking about things from the perspective of your mom: Is that really what *you'd* want to be doing after a long day of work? Respect means washing your own dishes; honor means washing hers, too.

In fact, pulling your own weight around the house is perhaps one of the most important issues of respect, and one that has lasting ramifications for your future romantic relationships. Of course, this doesn't necessarily become an issue *before* you get married, but conflicts over shared space, shared finances, and shared belongings can increase the longer a couple stays together. If you've consistently ignored the basic operations needed to make a home run smoothly while living with your parents, siblings, or roommates, there will be more battles to fight with Mr. Darcy when it comes time to create a home together. If he wants the fridge scrubbed weekly, fine. He can do it himself. But if the two of you have played Rock, Paper, Scissors to see who will take out the trash and you're the loser, then do it cheerfully before the Department of Toxic Substance Control comes along to quarantine your kitchen. Fair is fair.

Okay, so you're not even close to sharing a kitchen with Mr. Darcy yet. In fact, you're not even serious. All right, so you're not *dating*, period. But you *are* currently assessing his DP. How on earth do you gauge on a first date whether or not a guy respects his parents or pulls his weight around the house? Are you supposed to figure this out by how he wipes the crumbs off the tablecloth at the restaurant or kindly tells the waitress not to bother with a refill? Right. A bit unrealistic. It may take several dates and some carefully worded questions about family issues before you get even the slightest idea of who this guy is in relationship to family. But as you get to know him better, it's not hard to see how seriously he takes responsibilities at home.

Sure, Jane Austen's Darcy doesn't have to clean the toilets at Pemberley, but that's beside the point.

Communication

INTERPLANETARY POLITICS AND OTHER MATTERS

"I talked to [Lydia] repeatedly in the most serious manner, representing

*to her all the wickedness of what she had done, and all the
unhappiness she had brought on her family. If she heard me,
it was by good luck, for I am sure she did not listen."*

AUNT GARDINER, IN A LETTER TO ELIZABETH,
VOLUME THREE, CHAPTER TEN

You'd think that opening your mouth to say what's
on your mind would be as easy as breathing. After all,
words are the foundation of pretty much every activity the average girl could find to do in a day (try
e-mailing a friend without using words!). But somehow when it comes to communicating with family
members, the rules of language often break down
and you find yourself back to basic vowel sounds:
"Oh, uh . . ." Either you're so angry at your parents
or siblings that you can't speak, or you've given up on
ever being understood.

To make matters worse, listening to them sometimes feels like watching a foreign film without sub-
titles. You know they're making sense to themselves,
but you don't have a clue what planet they think
they're from. And even when you understand what
they're getting at, sometimes it's hard to care.

Listening to your parents or siblings sometimes requires the patience of Jane Bennet, but you feel more like Lizzy most of the time.

Yet even though Lizzy often has to hold her tongue around her foolish mother and sisters, she doesn't treat them like they're invisible. Lizzy listens when her mom demands her attention and responds with as much kindness as she can muster. She also steps in to censor Mrs. Bennet's unkind statements about other people, including Darcy.

Lizzy is on equal intellectual footing with her dad, however, so she can speak with more assurance of being understood. And yet she still struggles when she must communicate her fears about Lydia going off to Brighton. Overall, Lizzy picks her verbal battles carefully and doesn't engage in bickering sniper fire, even though she could easily win against every last member of her family except possibly Mr. Bennet.

She's not quite as careful in her earlier communications with Darcy, however. The phrase "conflict

management" comes to mind. If their first few
encounters are any indication, Lizzy and Darcy will
have some interesting communication issues to work
out once they finally get together.

For starters, their relationship begins with
verbal sparring—not the best of habits to form at the
beginning of a lifelong partner-
ship! Picture some of their interactions while Jane is sick at
Netherfield. Sure, much of the
dialogue is born out of the tension
created by their mutual attraction
in spite of their determination not to like each
other. But we also catch glimpses of Mr. Bennet's
ironic witticisms to his wife in what Lizzy says to
Darcy; and in turn we hear echoes of Darcy's arrogant aunt Lady Catherine de Bourgh in some of his
haughtier statements. Thus it's not merely Lizzy and
Darcy conversing in the drawing room after dinner;
it's the vastly different worlds of Longbourn and
Pemberley staging a standoff, with some saber-

> ⊜ ⊜ ⊜
> Mr. Darcy looked a little
> ashamed of his aunt's
> ill breeding, and made
> no answer.
>
> FROM *PRIDE AND
> PREJUDICE*

rattling thrown in. "*Your* defect is a propensity to hate every body," Lizzy announces archly, to which he responds with a smile, "And yours . . . is wilfully to misunderstand them." Yowch.

So their families haven't set the best example for conflict management. But that doesn't mean conflict itself is a bad thing. Disagreement is an inevitable part of two different people coming together. Managing your words and actions during times of conflict becomes an important cornerstone to the relationship. If, like Lizzy, you haven't had the best model when it comes to the fine art of fighting fair, you'll have some work to do in practicing helpful techniques when emotions are high, such as asking for a few moments by yourself to cool off.

Jane Austen herself would have been more than familiar with the conflict management technique found in Ephesians 4:26: "Don't let the sun go down while you are still angry," which calls to mind the scene of Darcy staying up all night writing a letter to Lizzy after she turns down his first marriage proposal. At the beginning of the letter, he is obviously furious at the manner of her rejection, but by the end he has worked through the emotion and is able to finish with "God bless you." Much later, after they are engaged, she assures him, "The letter, perhaps, began in bitterness, but it did not end so. The adieu is charity itself."

> ❋ ❋ ❋
> She was in no humour for conversation with any one but himself; and to him she had hardly courage to speak.
> FROM *PRIDE AND PREJUDICE*

We must not downplay the importance of Darcy's letter to Lizzy either. It's not just a matter of working through conflict; it's an important signal to Lizzy as to just exactly what sort of guy he is. He may not be the kind who is verbally eloquent about what he's thinking and feeling, like Wickham is, but that doesn't mean Darcy shuts down. Instead, he takes the time to articulate his inner thoughts by writing them down, something he's actually quite good at. He appears to value clear and honest communication in whatever form he can offer it. But more important, he values clear and honest communication with *her*.

That he would take the time to write to Lizzy is a key turning point in the story. She knows that he says very little to people like Miss Bingley but writes extensive letters to his sister, Georgiana. For him to write such a lengthy note to Lizzy means he treats her as on par with his sister, as someone worth opening his heart to, despite the fact that she's turned him down, possibly forever. He can't stand to have her think poorly of him. He's determined to work through this conflict somehow, even if it's only to clear his own name and reputation. He will do what he can to keep the lines of communication open.

What about *your* prospective Mr. Darcy? How well does he stay in touch with loved ones? When it comes to *Pride and Prejudice*, it's not hard to see what Mr. Darcy's attempts at communicating on paper have to say about him as a person and as a family guy. If ever circumstances keep him and Lizzy apart for any length of time during their marriage, we can be sure he will write her eloquent letters late into the night and profess all manner of lovely things that

probably shouldn't be repeated in public (e.g.,
"Dinner was desolate without you, dearest, loveliest
Elizabeth" [gasp!]). Yep, he's a keeper.

And how about you? How well do you stay in touch
with your family when circumstances keep you apart? Do
you communicate your love for them through phone
calls, e-mails, letters, birthday gifts? What do those
attempts at staying in touch say about you?

Another aspect of communication that doesn't
seem important to mention but is perhaps the hard-
est to master is the tricky job of *listening* when our
family members get up the courage to tackle a subject
that's near to our hearts, such as, say, our boyfriend.
Often we're tempted to push our parents away, especially if they haven't had exactly the most pristine
history themselves when it comes to romance. But in
doing so we could be missing out on some vitally
important warnings or encouragements.

In Lizzy's case, she knows good advice when she
hears it (especially if it's from her aunt Gardiner, for
example), and she isn't afraid to keep the lines of

communication open with the ones she loves. It's not hard to see how that will eventually pay off in her relationship with Darcy down the road. When he has difficult things to express, she'll be ready to listen, and vice versa.

It's a worthy goal. In the end, if we don't get a handle on healthy communication as a basic function of human existence, we put our romantic relationships at risk. All of the communication habits, healthy or unhealthy, that we form in our family are exactly the patterns of behavior we fall into when we have crucial things to discuss with Darcy.

> "Will you be very angry with me, my dear Lizzy, if I take this opportunity of saying (what I was never bold enough to say before) how much I like him."
>
> MRS. GARDINER, IN A LETTER TO LIZZY ABOUT DARCY

Integrity

HOW TO SPOT THE MULTIPLE-PERSONALITY BOYFRIEND

> *"You shall not, for the sake of one individual, change the meaning of principle and integrity."*
>
> ELIZABETH TO JANE BENNET, VOLUME TWO, CHAPTER ONE

Integrity is a dusty old word, but it's absolutely vital to the health of your family relationships. It basically means not living a double life in which you act one way at home and another way at school or with your friends. This is bigger than simply not lying to your parents about where you were after school or about what happened to your science report. It's more like not having a multiple personality disorder in which you become a different person from one setting to the next: the dutiful daughter at home, the sassy chick with friends, the spotless saint at youth group, the vixen around guys.

And what about your Number One Crush? How do you gauge *his* integrity? Here's where Lizzy fails in her judgment at first, particularly in regard to Wickham. We learn from Darcy's letter that Wickham never showed his real self around Darcy's dad, which is why he stayed in Mr. Darcy Sr.'s good graces. Wickham is a charmer. He can pretend to be the dutiful "son" and get away with it. The young Darcy, on the other hand, remains himself from one setting to another. Though he doesn't agree with his father's confidence in Wickham's character, Darcy will honor his father's wishes that Wickham be taken care of. He isn't going to say yes to his father's instructions and then do the opposite when the old man isn't looking. Darcy is the same person around his father that he is everywhere else. Wickham is not. We can only imagine how this lack of integrity will play itself out in his marriage to Lydia.

> "But we are none of us consistent."
> MR. WICKHAM

We see this same lack of integrity in the Bingley sisters, who are nicer to Jane when their brother is around than when he's gone. We can assume it's because they want to stay in their brother's good graces. The minute he turns his back, they roll their eyes and plot to separate Jane and Bingley as soon as possible. They act one way around their brother and a completely different way around each other. If this is the sort of pattern they develop with the guy in their family, what does that mean for their (in Miss Bingley's case, future) husbands?

Part of maintaining your integrity in the family setting—of being the same person at home that you are elsewhere—is to spend quality time with your parents and siblings. Sure, Caroline Bingley spends lots of time with her "dear brother." But is it really time well spent? Picture her during the evenings at Netherfield when Jane is sick. Lizzy watches with interest how little of substance is actually said or done among these bored, wealthy young people. If anything, their relationships are deteriorating rather than being strengthened by the way they choose to spend their time together. Lizzy also notes that Darcy, for want of something worthwhile to do, writes letters to his sister rather than sitting around gossiping.

And what about you? Do you shut down when your family is around? Do you turn on the TV, zone out in front of the computer, call your friends, sulk in your room, leave the dinner table as quickly as possible? Yes, we need alone time, as Lizzy well knows. But part of building strong ties to family is

taking the time to get to know them as unique indi-
viduals, not just as "sister" or "dad." As Philippians
2:4 says, "Don't look out only for your own interests, but take an interest in others,
too."

So rather than hollering bye to
your mom while snatching a
Pop-Tart and dashing out the door
in the morning, spend a little less time in the bathroom for once and actually sit down at the breakfast
table. Ask what she's got going on for the day. It's the
fine art of treasuring rather than wasting opportunities to spend time with the people who let you live at
home for free. Quality time with family takes work,
but it helps you get to know them better, build
memories, strengthen ties, keep each other company,
accomplish projects, and find things you have in
common.

> "Such squeamish youths
> as cannot bear to be
> connected with a little
> absurdity, are not
> worth a regret."
> MR. BENNET TO LIZZY

The more meaningful time you spend at home,
the less tempting it will be to act like a different
person when you're somewhere else.

When It's All Said and Done

You won't always be at Longbourn, surrounded by the home culture of whatever Bennets God gave you.

⊙ ⊛ ⊙

DEAR SIR,

I must trouble you once more for congratulations. Elizabeth will soon be the wife of Mr. Darcy. Console Lady Catherine as well as you can. But, if I were you, I would stand by the nephew. He has more to give.

MR. BENNET'S LETTER TO MR. COLLINS

But the habits you develop in your family relationships—especially when it comes to respect, communication, and integrity—influence your romantic attachments down the road. How will this knowledge change the way you interact with your family from now on?

Part Three

FRIENDS

Part Three

FRIENDS

"You appear to me, Mr. Darcy, to allow nothing for the influence
of friendship and affection."

ELIZABETH BENNET, VOLUME ONE, CHAPTER TEN

It's probably happened to you. One minute you and
your best friend are inseparable. You're together
every weekend, shopping, watching chick flicks, and
snarfing Ben & Jerry's. You spend hours analyzing
your respective love interests and call each other the
minute your crush says hello at the coffeehouse. ("So

was he like, 'Hello, hot mama,' or like, 'Hello, I'm just being polite'?")

But the next minute, along comes some guy named Bingley and your best friend drops off the face of the planet. It's like you never existed. Without prior notification, you find yourself alone on a Friday night, scooping chocolate-mocha-crunch out of a carton and watching *Friends* reruns.

Dating relationships have tremendous power to alienate us from others, as we've all experienced at one point or another. Some of us have been the ones guilty of abandoning our friends when our own Mr. Marvelous comes along (including this author—sorry, everyone). What we forget is that our friends are a crucial part of our identity. Let's face it: Who *else* has seen us on a bad hair day and *still* loves us (besides Mom)?

Though we don't like to think along these lines, we're accountable to our friends when it comes to dating, just as we're accountable to our family. The choices we make in romance affect everyone who has

ever loved us, which is why we need to take friendships into account in the dating game.

Think *Lydia* again. When the youngest Bennet
sister runs off with Wickham, her uncle Gardiner
says, "Could he expect that her friends would not
step forward?" In other words, Lydia is part of a tight
community that keeps track of its own, though Mr.
and Mrs. Bennet have been negligent enough. She
can't stray far before the local posse goes on the
hunt. Unfortunately, Wickham is sharp enough to
figure this out. He ensures that the couple secretly
disappears so no one can track them down. A huge
amount of energy and money are expended before
Lydia is restored—as best as possible under the
circumstances—to her friends and family.

But well before Lydia runs away with Wickham,
she begins to make the break from her home life,
especially from her sister Kitty, who has always been
her closest confidant. Lydia aligns herself instead
with the flighty young Mrs. Forster, the wife of the
colonel of Wickham's regiment, and chooses that

friendship over the older, more stable ones she's had all her life. When Mrs. Forster invites Lydia to join her in Brighton with the regiment, Lydia ignores Kitty's misery and instead celebrates her success. The two girls are separated by Lydia's choice, a separation that becomes permanent when she finally elopes with Wickham.

Admittedly, there's a certain amount of separation that happens eventually in all friendships, even the healthy ones, especially when one friend becomes romantically involved with a guy. Lizzy experiences this when it comes to her good friend Charlotte Lucas, whom Jane Austen describes as "a sensible, intelligent young woman." Lizzy and Charlotte are a classic example of how friendships can change when one or the other forms a romantic attachment—well, shall we say, when one or the other forms an *attachment*, period. Charlotte is not the romantic type. But her bewildering decision to marry Mr. Collins puts a strain on her friendship with Lizzy that changes it forever.

Thankfully, though, Lizzy also has Jane to turn to

as both a sister *and* a friend. They've learned to rely on each other as the only sane representatives of the female species in the crazy Bennet household, though their personalities are quite different. Lizzy is lively, assertive, and quick to form judgments, while Jane is mild, sweet, and thinks everyone is innocent till proven guilty (and even then, she believes there has probably been some mistake). When one is sad or hurt, the other is too. They share their most intimate secrets, rely on each other's wisdom, pass the Kleenex, and stand up for each other against the ridiculous demands of their mother and sisters. Their friendship is part of their identity; what happens to one, especially when it comes to their love interests, affects the other.

Your girlfriends form an important part of your identity too—a role that grows stronger the older you get and the farther you move away from the home circle. While *Friends* and Bridget Jones aren't perhaps the best examples, you get the picture: Life out in the big, bad world is awfully lonely without roommates, coworkers, and church friends to fill the gap and help you establish a sense of identity once you're out on your own. Needless to say, the closer you are to your girlfriends, the greater the impact of your dating relationship on the sisterhood.

> ◉ ◉ ◉
>
> Among his own connections he was esteemed and valued— that even Wickham had allowed him merit as a brother, and that she had often heard him speak so affectionately of his sister as to prove him capable of some amiable feeling.
>
> LIZZY,
> REFLECTING ON DARCY'S CHARACTER

Friendship plays a role in Mr. Darcy's identity too. Unless he lives under a rock, your guy has at least a few close friends with whom he shares hobbies, interests, and take-out pizza on the weekends. What *do* guys talk about when they get together, anyway? When Mr. Darcy busts up laughing at some idiotic thing Mr. Bingley just said, what's going on there? Weird guy stuff, that's what. And don't bother trying to figure it out. It's enough to know they've been friends for years and years and will probably be friends for life. Just make sure Bingley signs a contract not to trash your car during the wedding.

Okay, so Jane Austen's Bingley would never do

that. (There weren't cars in Regency England, for one thing, but that's beside the point.) Bingley and Darcy are strong friends, and both take a keen interest in the health and welfare of the other. Yes, Darcy is a bit heavy-handed when it comes to taking care of Bingley, especially in regard to Jane. All right, Darcy is downright *wrong*. But he really believes he's keeping Bingley and Jane apart for the best, out of genuine concern for his friend. He doesn't want to see him get hurt, either by Jane's rejection of him—because she doesn't appear to favor him in any particular way—or by the baseness of her relations, which might drag Bingley's reputation down in society. Sure, Darcy is a snob. But he's an honest snob.

The Bible says, "There are 'friends' who destroy each other, but a real friend sticks closer than a brother" (Proverbs 18:24). If the Mr. Darcy you're interested in has close friendships with good guys

> "It does not often happen that the interference of friends will persuade a young man of independent fortune to think no more of a girl, whom he was violently in love with only a few days before."
>
> LIZZY TO HER AUNT, ON JANE'S LOSS OF BINGLEY'S ATTENTIONS

who stand by him when things get tough, there's something important going on. His friends recognize something about his character that's worth hanging on to. He doesn't try to climb over them to get to the top of the pack. He genuinely cares about what's going on in their lives.

In short, guys like Darcy and Bingley are the guys you want to date. And not just because they're hot. Romance is more than just physical attraction; it's also friendship. If your Mr. Darcy is a good friend to others, then he'll be a good friend to you.

The reverse is also true: Your own friendships become the proving ground for how good a friend you'll be to *him*. What you discover in the dating game is that friends play a larger role in your life than you often give them credit for. And whether you're dating or single, building strong, healthy friendships is one of the ways you grow into the kind of woman who is able to have a strong, healthy romance.

How we measure or assess the health of our friendships is similar to how we measure the health of our family relationships, which is why we won't spend as much time discussing them in this chapter. We've already covered much of the same ground. But it's important to see how the issues of communication, respect, and integrity (in this case, loyalty) apply to our friendships—and to Darcy's too.

Communication

KEEPING IN TOUCH WITH THE SISTERHOOD (FOR YOUR OWN SANITY)

> *Elizabeth soon heard from her friend [Charlotte]; and their correspondence was as regular and frequent as it had ever been; that it should be equally unreserved was impossible. Elizabeth could never address her without feeling that all the comfort of intimacy was over, and, though determined not to slacken as a correspondent, it was for the sake of what had been, rather than what was.*
>
> *Pride and Prejudice*, PART TWO, CHAPTER THREE

When it comes to communication with friends while we're dating someone, the Love Nest Syndrome is unfortunately all too common. When that happens, we make room enough in our lives for only one person and shut out everyone else. But this can be a dangerous game that sets us up for loneliness and regret down the road if we don't stay in touch with our friends.

You know what it feels like to be on the receiving end of a friend's Love Nest behavior, right? One of the toughest things to communicate to a friend is concern for how her boyfriend is having a negative impact on her life. We all have at least one friend who is dating a guy who is just not right for her. It's obvious to everybody, but no one has the guts to say anything. At what point do you confront your friend? How do you broach the subject without pushing her away?

Now turn the tables. What if *you're* the one who's hooked up with a questionable character? Will you listen when your friends offer advice? Have you cultivated the kinds of friendships in which the sisterhood can be honest with you about things you

> At such a time, much might have been said, and silence was very awkward. She wanted to talk, but there seemed an embargo on every subject.
>
> ELIZABETH, AFTER DISCOVERING DARCY'S HELP WITH LYDIA

don't necessarily want to hear? We become alienated from our friends when we fail to listen to what they have to say. Genuine listening is an art form that takes patience and humility, especially in the sticky arena of romance.

Too often when things fall apart in our dating relationships, as they usually do, we've cut off communication with those who would've been willing to help carry our emotional burdens, or at least to pass the Kleenex. We need our friends because ultimately our adorable Mr. Darcy will never be able to fulfill all our needs, as much as he might fit all the criteria we've laid out for the perfect partner. There are some things he just can't do that our girlfriends, sisters—even mothers and mentors—can.

This doesn't mean we ditch Darcy on the weekends once we realize just how far short he falls from fulfilling all our social, relational, or emotional needs. But it does mean that we cultivate those other relationships along the way. We need input from the female perspective, a sisterly shoulder to cry on, the womanly wisdom of our older aunts and clever cousins. If we've cut off everyone who cared about us before, who will we turn to?

We can't overlook our guy friends, either, the ones we talk to when Darcy is acting weird. Sometimes guys can see through their own kind better than we ever can, and they are able to give a pretty good assessment of what's going on. For Lizzy, one such friend is Darcy's cousin, Colonel Fitzwilliam. Actually, we begin to wonder if she has a bit of a crush on him, posing an interesting conundrum for those of us who are rooting for Darcy. In our own relationships, we must be careful not to turn our affections to other guys when Darcy is being ridiculous. Our male friends are there to support us, not to get sucked into some twisted love triangle. The smart ones, like Colonel Fitzwilliam, will wisely keep their distance while offering whatever brotherly advice they can.

So how do you maintain close communication with your friends while dating The Most Amazing

Guy on Earth? All the obvious ways come to mind. Phone calls are quick ways to say, "You're still important to me," as well as to catch your friends up on your life. And remember to listen to what's going on in their lives too; as tempted as you may be to run through the Top One Hundred Reasons I Love Mr. Darcy, your friends actually have other stuff they care about. No, seriously. You also need to take time away from the Love Nest to go out for coffee with the sisterhood or host a chick-flick marathon some weekend. This may take some planning ahead, but the effort is worth it.

Another important aspect of communication with friends, as we discussed in the chapter on family, is staying in touch through the written word, whether through snail mail or e-mail. It's believed that *Pride and Prejudice* initially was written as a series of letters, or as an epistolary novel. We learn a lot about the characters and their relationships to one another by the quantity and quality of their long-distance communications. After marrying Mr. Collins, Charlotte requests that

Lizzy keep up the correspondence and come visit her. Lizzy doesn't say, "Well, it's your own stupid fault for marrying him. You're on your own, girlfriend." No, she recognizes that Charlotte sees their communications as something of a lifeline, a way to keep sane when Mr. Collins is driving her crazy. And Lizzy cares enough about her friend to stay in touch, even though their relationship is forever changed.

Jane and Lizzy write letters continually too, whenever they're separated. For Jane, it's a way to process her feelings for Bingley and get a level-headed perspective on the Bingleys' treatment of her. For Lizzy, it's a crucial connection to her closest friend, without whom the Bennet household seems like one *Jerry Springer* episode after another. Lydia, by contrast, fails to stay in touch with her family once she heads off to Brighton. Her letters are short, fluffy, and infrequent. Based on their letter writing alone,

> Between Elizabeth and Charlotte there was a restraint which kept them mutually silent on the subject; and Elizabeth felt persuaded that no real confidence could ever subsist between them again.
>
> REGARDING CHARLOTTE'S MARRIAGE TO MR. COLLINS

it's easy to recognize which of the Bennet sisters are most capable of creating lasting friendships and, consequently, establishing healthy romance.

"I long to see you again," writes one of the authors of the New Testament, "for I remember your tears as we parted. And I will be filled with joy when we are together again" (2 Timothy 1:4). The written word is an important way to document our feelings and experiences in friendship. We can look back and remember how much a friend meant to us and the important role they've played in our lives.

Good friends are hard to find and easy to lose through neglect. Communication keeps the friendship alive.

~

Respect

WHAT HIS FRIENDSHIPS INDICATE ABOUT HOW HE'LL TREAT YOU

> *Between [Bingley] and Darcy there was a very steady friendship,*
> *in spite of a great opposition of character.*
> *Pride and Prejudice*, VOLUME ONE, CHAPTER FOUR

My, how we love Bingley! If he weren't already taken by Jane, we'd be tempted to fall for him ourselves.

Darcy and Bingley's friendship is built upon a mutual respect that draws them together in spite of Bingley's annoying sisters. We're not sure exactly how these guys met, but we catch rather humorous glimpses of why they get along: Bingley likes having someone around who will guide and direct him, while Darcy is something of a control freak who likes being cruise director for someone so compliant.

> "Oh! yes," said Elizabeth drily—"Mr. Darcy is uncommonly kind to Mr. Bingley, and takes a prodigious deal of care of him."
> "Care of him!—Yes, I really believe Darcy does take care of him in those points where he most wants care."
>
> LIZZY AND COLONEL FITZWILLIAM

It's a friendship Lizzy at first finds outrageous, especially since it interferes with the happiness of her own sister. But eventually, after she becomes engaged to Mr. Darcy, she finds it amusing—though she doesn't dare laugh at Darcy about it, because he has "yet to learn to be laught at." The most important thing is that she realizes Bingley can stand up for himself when he applies enough energy and will-power, and ultimately, Darcy will act in his friend's best interest. Their respect for each other proves to be the strong foundation that remains unshaken even when tough situations rock the friendship.

Lizzy, too, treats her friends with respect, even when they go off the deep end and do idiotic things like marry creepy cousins of hers. She may not agree with Charlotte's decision to become Mrs. Collins, for example, but she doesn't ditch the relationship. Lizzy is still able to esteem her friend even though their friendship is inevitably altered by Charlotte's choice.

> And to the pang of a friend disgracing herself and sunk in her esteem, was added the distressing conviction that it was impossible for that friend to be tolerably happy in the lot she had chosen.
>
> LIZZY,
> REGARDING CHARLOTTE'S
> MARRIAGE TO COLLINS

When it comes to Lizzy and Jane's friendship, theirs is the kind that weathers differences in personality. They're able to respect each other's strengths and aren't afraid to comment on each other's weaknesses. Though Lizzy may tease Jane for always looking on the bright side, she recognizes how beneficial it can be to have such an upbeat attitude. And though Jane may censure Lizzy for making snap judgments about people like Miss Bingley, she acknowledges when Lizzy's been right. Together they're able to keep each other balanced, especially when the Bennet household seems on the brink of lunacy.

So Lizzy's friendships are built upon genuine respect. She doesn't take a superior attitude and distance herself from Charlotte or Jane when they make choices she disapproves of. She doesn't strive to be the chick in charge of the sisterhood by using her wit to belittle and humble others. Yes, she speaks her mind, but only to express loving concern for her friends, not to sneer.

How many of our own friendships echo those of Lizzy and Jane, and Darcy and Bingley in regard to mutual respect? If we're honest, very few. Sometimes our friends are so wrapped up in their selfish little worlds that they only create more chaos in our lives. And sometimes *we're* so wrapped up in our own stuff that we fail to see *them* as anything more than a useful ride to the mall or a handy companion when we're bored. It's easy to ditch our friends when they show even the tiniest character flaw or fail to be useful anymore.

Ephesians 4:2 says, "Be patient with each other, making allowance for each other's faults because of your love." Lasting friendships are built on more than mere convenience. Genuine friends go out of their way to honor and take care of each other, even when the prospect of romance comes along.

Loyalty

THE ART OF TOUGHING IT OUT WHEN THINGS GET WEIRD

> *"Mr. Wickham is blessed with such happy manners as may ensure his making friends—whether he may be equally capable of retaining them, is less certain."*
>
> MR. DARCY TO ELIZABETH, VOLUME ONE, CHAPTER EIGHTEEN

We've all had a friend (or former friend) who seems to have a split personality from one setting to another. It's like she lives a double life. When she's with you, she's nice and shares all kinds of secrets. But get her in a room full of popular people she wants to impress, and nobody would have a clue she'd ever even met you before.

The same issue of integrity that we discussed in the chapter about family applies to friendships, too. It's about being the same person from one setting to another, from one relationship to another. Except within friendships, the concept of integrity is best expressed as *loyalty*: sticking by your friend no matter what's going on in his or her life, or in yours.

> ● ◉ ●
> "Can his most intimate friends be so excessively deceived in him? oh! no."
> JANE TO LIZZY, IN REFERENCE TO WHAT THEY'VE LEARNED ABOUT DARCY FROM WICKHAM

The former friendship of Wickham to Darcy shows disloyalty at its worst. We learn from Wickham that he and Darcy grew up together: "We were born in the same parish, within the same park, the greatest part of our youth was passed together; inmates of the same house, sharing the same amusements, objects of the same parental care." But in Darcy's letter we hear the rest of the story. Wickham has been disloyal to his childhood friend in every possible way—dishonoring the memory of Darcy's father, squandering Darcy's money, and almost eloping with Darcy's sister.

But Wickham's lack of integrity goes even one step further. When describing to Lizzy what happened in his friendship with Darcy, Wickham begins a malicious rumor about how Darcy cheated him out of the "living" (church position) he should have been given. The rumor eventually spreads to the entire community of Meryton, making Darcy look like a villain. Proverbs 16:28 sums up Wickham's character perfectly: "A troublemaker plants seeds of strife; gossip separates the best of friends."

Loyalty means building a friendship that's based on trust. When our friend tells us to keep something confidential, we do. But despite the fact that we may have been burned over and over by the malicious rumors that our so-called friends have started, we, too, are often tempted to tell other people things our friends have told us in secret. Loyalty keeps us from gossiping about them behind their backs.

Loyalty also helps us stick by our friends even when their choices or their lifestyles don't mesh with ours. Miss Bingley, for example, is quick to shake off her friendship with Jane when it requires her to associate with Jane's lower-class relatives. By contrast, Lizzy doesn't ditch Charlotte just because her friend has made what she feels is a foolish decision to marry Mr. Collins. Lizzy still maintains the friendship "for the sake of what had been"—proving herself to be a loyal and persevering friend. As Proverbs 17:17 says, "A friend is always loyal, and a brother is born to help in time of need." Lizzy demonstrates what it means to stick by your friends even when things aren't going so well between you.

> ☉ ☉ ☉
> "My dearest Lizzy will, I am sure, be incapable of triumphing in her better judgment, at my expense, when I confess myself to have been entirely deceived in Miss Bingley's regard for me."
>
> JANE,
> IN A LETTER TO LIZZY

It's not hard to see how loyalty in friendship prepares you for loyalty in your dating relationships down the road.

There will be days when Darcy drives you crazy or makes foolish decisions. If you're in the habit of dropping your friends whenever the same happens with them, you'll never learn what it means to tough it out in romance.

When It's All Said and Done

"Were it for nothing but [Darcy's] love of you, I must always have esteemed him; but now, as Bingley's friend and your husband, there can be only Bingley and yourself more dear to me."

JANE BENNET TO ELIZABETH, VOLUME THREE, CHAPTER SEVENTEEN

It's a trick to integrate your friendships into your life when you're dating Mr. Darcy. It takes effort on both parts to leave the Love Nest now and then in order to get to know each other's friends. Spending time with each of them is a good place to start. You'll also want to observe how Darcy and his friends interact with each other, keeping in mind that guys build friendships around the activities they like to do together, such as sports, travel, and other hobbies. Pay attention to the way they communicate too. Do they discuss the important stuff in life, such as family issues, faith, sins or struggles, or their goals and dreams?

You will not always be in Meryton, surrounded by the Janes and Charlottes God gave you. But the habits you develop in your friendships—especially when it comes to communication, respect, and loyalty—influence your romantic attachments down the road. How will this knowledge change the way you interact with your friends from now on?

Part Four

FAITH

Part Four

"I knew that Mr. Wickham ought not to be a clergyman."

Mr. Darcy in his letter to Elizabeth,
Volume Two, Chapter Twelve

The guy is schmoozing big-time, and you're falling
for it. And why not? He's hot, friendly, intelligent,
obviously flirting with you—and he talks about
church. Granted, it's rather casually tossed into the
conversation now and then ("last week, just as I was
getting out of church," etc.), but still, it's a sign.

He's a guy with deep conviction, good principles, and healthy habits, the kind of person who will treat you like a princess and never intentionally hurt you or anyone else. Right?

Take care, girlfriend. *Any*body can talk about church; and *any*body can go to church, even Wickham. Just because a guy steps inside the building for an hour on Sunday morning (or talks like he does) doesn't mean he follows Jesus during the other hundred and sixty-seven hours of the week. You need to consider: "Does this guy walk his talk? He speaks all kinds of religious language, but is he really living like he believes it?" Jesus says, "Just as you can identify a tree by its fruit, so you can identify people by their actions" (Matthew 7:20). You want a guy who steadily shows by his outward behavior that he belongs to God for the long-term, even when you're not looking.

> ● ● ●
>
> For herself, she was humbled; but she was proud of him. Proud that in a cause of compassion and honour, he had been able to get the better of himself.
>
> LIZZY REFLECTING ON DARCY'S SELF-SACRIFICING BEHAVIOR TOWARD WICKHAM AND LYDIA

We've already said that the character of your prospective Darcy is largely shaped and influenced by his relationships with family and friends. But his character is also, and most importantly, shaped by his relationship with God. God gave him a unique personality and spirit that only God truly understands the depths of. From the standpoint of the Christian faith, a person is only complete when he recognizes the presence and role of God in his life. Until then, he is a shadow of himself, a mere echo of all that God intends him to be. Faith gives him a solid identity.

The same is true for you. Your relationship with God (or lack thereof?) is the defining aspect of your character—more important than your relationships with family and friends. God is the one who created you, and he, as the Author of the great story of humankind, has given you a role as one of the characters.

The Christian faith sees all of history as a divine romance in which every human character is in the process of being wooed back to the loving heart of God. From the beginning, people turned their backs on God, an act that separated us from him forever until Jesus came. God's Son chose to suffer the indignity of taking on human form—and even went so far as to sacrifice his very life—so that we would no longer be separated from God except by our own hard-heartedness. God has been wooing us back ever since.

The plot sounds suspiciously familiar, come to think of it. Where have we heard it recently? Two characters become separated at the beginning of their relationship, have a falling out, and aren't able to come together again until one of them makes a great sacrifice for the sake of the beloved, eventually wooing her back again. . . .

Wait! Of course!

Okay, so this could be reading into things. It may seem ridiculous to speak of faith in Jane Austen's novels when the author herself doesn't seem to address the issue. And yet it's an inescapable theme that, upon further study, we find woven through her stories in the shape of characters who, by their foolishness or wisdom in romance, become living parables of our relationship with God. It's a parallel that's unavoidable in the genre of romance in general, and in romantic comedy in particular, because at the heart of the universe is a divine romance with a happy ending (the true definition of comedy).

Faith is rarely discussed in *Pride and Prejudice* except in the negative examples of Mary Bennet and Mr. Collins, whose comments are intended to make us wince and snort with laughter at the same time. It's as though Jane Austen is making fun of spiritual people. Sure, the words "religious" and "Christian" pop up now and then, but the concept of the characters having a personal relationship with God isn't even alluded to. It'd be very easy to argue that there's nothing Christian about these stories at all.

> ● ● ●
>
> They found Mary, as usual, deep in the study of thorough bass and human nature; and had some new extracts to admire, and some new observations of thread-bare morality to listen to.
>
> FROM *PRIDE AND PREJUDICE*

But let's consider Jane Austen herself. Jane
lived in a time when the Christian faith was taken for
granted. She likely felt no need to reference or lay
out the basic beliefs of Christianity in her writings
because her readers would have known them, at least
intellectually.

Jane was also a minister's daughter, which meant
that church, prayer, and Bible study were integral to
her life. Among the original papers and documents
we still have from her collection are several prayers
she wrote for her family for use during evening devotions when her father wasn't there to lead them.
Some of the prayers are quoted later in this book in
the Guide to Reflection.

It could be argued that her prayers indicate that
she felt a personal *experience* of God to be central to
the life of faith, even if the language of having a
personal *relationship* with God would have sounded
foreign to her (as foreign as, say, having a personal
relationship with the king of England). The founda-
tional beliefs of the Anglican church[6] affirm that

living the Christian life is more than just attending worship on Sunday morning. Living as a Christian means you accept the free gift of salvation and forgiveness that Jesus offers and you choose to follow in his footsteps for the rest of your life. You no longer serve yourself first: God is first and others are second.

Jane may have echoed the formal language of the Church of England to express our need for forgiveness through Jesus Christ, but her prayers are uniquely focused on the need to acknowledge our sin and turn to him.

We get hints of faith in her fiction, particularly in the character development of her main heroes and heroines. As one writer has noted, "Her fictional characters are either thoughtful and religious, or heedless and irreligious."[7] In other words, her characters either take the responsibility of faith seriously or they don't, and the reader knows exactly which attitude is the most heroic.

A great example of taking faith seriously occurs

in *Sense and Sensibility*. When Marianne Dashwood
recovers from her illness, she realizes with shame that
she has messed up *big*-time—not just in poor judgment, but in immodesty, disrespect of others, and
lack of openness with her loved ones. She states that,
from here on out, she will curb her behavior "by
religion, by reason, by constant employment."[8] The
sensible boundaries that the Christian faith gives will
be the basis for her behavior from now on.

Here it's important to say that when we talk
about the Christian faith, we mean more than just
the *religion*. We mean the *relationship* we have with God.
Religion is the framework of moral obligations that
guide our thoughts, speech, and actions. As a
member of the church, Jane Austen was emphatically
religious, and rightly so. Religion is important, but
we must never forget that religion is merely the
outward expression of the inward reality that we have
a relationship with the living God of the universe.

Through her fictional characters, Jane Austen
seems to suggest that faith plays a key role in our

romantic relationships. We get the sense that what Marianne Dashwood is beginning to grasp—and Lydia Bennet is not—is that faith keeps us from putting one of two people, Self or Boyfriend, on the throne of our lives instead of the God who deserves to be there.

Let's start with what happens when you put Self on the throne. Elevating your own needs, wants, and desires above everybody else makes you the false queen of a little universe that doesn't exist. Once again, we think of Lydia's behavior toward her friends and family, even before she runs off with Wickham. Because her mother has spoiled her, Lydia thinks she's entitled to get what she wants. She doesn't care a bit that her words and actions hurt her family or lower their reputation in the eyes of the community. When we look at Lydia, it's clear that making an idol of ourselves only leads to one big mess after another. Know anyone like that? Yep, we all do.

So then there's the problem of putting your boyfriend on the throne of your life. This makes *him* the false king of yet another little universe that doesn't exist. Again, think of the example of Lydia: "There is but one man in the world I love, and he is an angel," she writes in her last note to Mrs. Forster before she runs away. Wickham? An *angel*? Ha! And yet how many of *us* have thought our own Number One Guy was beyond perfect? When we put our boyfriend on a high pedestal, we risk worshipping him as yet another idol. He will only disappoint us, just as Wickham surely disappointed Lydia within a matter of months (weeks? days?) after they ran away together.

There's a reason we're not to put Self or Boyfriend on the throne of our lives: Without God, we ultimately serve ourselves rather than others, bringing pain rather than joy. If you put yourself on the throne, you become a slave to your own desires, many of which are unhealthy, self-obsessed, and destructive. And if you put Darcy on the throne, you become either codependent—unable to function without him—or you become disappointed and resentful that he isn't living up to your Superman expectations.

Once we put the love of God in its proper place in our lives—number one—then we are better able to love others. That's the principle behind what Jesus says are the two greatest commandments: "Love the LORD your God with all your heart, all your soul, and all your mind" and "Love your neighbor as yourself" (Matthew 22:37-38). Love for God comes first, enabling us to better love ourselves and others.

The other thing that happens when we put God on the throne of our lives is that we're better able to survive when all other relationships fail us, including when we fail ourselves. When everything else falls apart and we are alone in the world, God is still there. Our universe doesn't disintegrate.

So the love of God comes first in our lives. But what does this have to do with Mr. Darcy and Elizabeth Bennet? Well, there are two aspects of faith that come through in their story and from which we can learn some important tips. The first is righteousness and the second is grace.

Righteousness

JUDGING A BOOK BY ITS COVER (AND OTHER PITFALLS)

> *Proud and repulsive as were [Darcy's] manners, she had never, in the*
> *whole course of their acquaintance, an acquaintance which had latterly*
> *brought them much together, and given her a sort of intimacy with his ways,*
> *seen any thing that betrayed him to be unprincipled or unjust—any thing*
> *that spoke him of irreligious or immoral habits.*
>
> *Pride and Prejudice*, VOLUME TWO, CHAPTER THIRTEEN

At first glance, it seems as though Jane Austen is constantly poking fun at the "righteousness" of her "religious" characters. And she is! There's nothing more ridiculous than someone who is trying to sound spiritual but clearly only wants to make him- or herself look good. Mary Bennet and Mr. Collins are prime examples.

First, we see Mary trying to distinguish herself in some way from her sisters by spending her time in "holy" pursuits like reading sermons and offering religious commentary on what others are doing. When Lydia elopes with Wickham, Mary says to Lizzy, "This is a most unfortunate affair; and will probably be much talked of. But we must stem the tide of malice, and pour into the wounded bosoms of each other, the balm of sisterly consolation." (The *what*?) She then blathers on, "Unhappy as the event must be for Lydia, we may draw from it this useful lesson. . . ." Blah, blah, blah. Lizzy is astonished that Mary is so unfeeling as to make a lesson out of their sister's mistake rather than grieve over it. On a good day, the rest of us would be tempted to snarl, "Look, Miss Perfect, take your sisterly consolation somewhere else!"

Then there's Mr. Collins, the only clergyman in the story, who is hardly someone Jane Austen wants us to like, admire, or imitate. His letter to Mr. Bennet after Lydia's elopement is self-righteousness at its most absurd. (Funny how Lydia's behavior brings out the worst in everyone else!) Mr. Bennet reads aloud from the letter Mr. Collins sent: "You ought certainly to forgive them, as a Christian, but never to admit them in your sight, or allow their names to be mentioned in your hearing." And then

Mr. Bennet adds in amused astonishment, "*That* is his notion of Christian forgiveness!" You catch the joke. The reader is supposed to recognize that the *truly* Christian response to Lydia's behavior would be to offer her grace and forgiveness she doesn't deserve, just as God has done for us.

So there's obviously a difference between the *self*-righteousness of people like Mary Bennet and Mr. Collins, who think they're better than everyone else, as compared to the outward-focused righteousness of someone like Mr. Darcy, who sacrifices a great deal of time and energy to take care of people he loves. Mary and Mr. Collins treat the sin of others as something to stay away from, at worst, and something to learn from, at best. Their religious expression is not based on a loving concern for others, but on a paranoid concern for their own moral cleanliness.

It's easy to see that Mr. Collins's pastoral advice and Mary's "moral extractions" are empty of genuine love and concern for Lydia. But the reader knows who the truly righteous people in the story are. Mary and Mr. Collins can say all the pious things they want: Elizabeth and Darcy will take action, if at all possible. "Dear children," writes one of the authors of the New Testament, "let's not merely say that we love each other; let us show the truth by our actions" (1 John 3:18). Actions rather than words are the truest test of our inner character.

> ⊙ ⊜ ⊙
> "I admire the activity of your benevolence, but every impulse of feeling should be guided by reason."
> MARY, IN RESPONSE TO LIZZY'S DESIRE TO WALK TO NETHERFIELD TO LOOK AFTER JANE

God is present behind the curtain of every scene in your life, and your awareness of his presence determines how you "act" with the other characters around you—your family, friends, and boyfriend included. This has nothing to do with trying to win God's approval, as so many people seem to think. We already have God's approval once we've committed our lives to Christ. No, we seek to love and serve others because it's the least we can do out of gratitude for God's love for us. Honoring God through our righteous behavior becomes a thrill and a delight rather than a boring duty.

As we said in the opening chapter, there is a higher rule or law that guides our speech and actions in all of our relationships, a law that says we are responsible for the pain others experience as a result of our selfish behavior. We will deal with the consequences someday—if not in this lifetime then certainly when we are face-to-face with God. We are accountable to God for the way our actions might hurt those who love us best.

This is why God has laid out rules of behavior that are the best possible plan for taking care of our beloved Darcy—and everyone else we love, including ourselves. In Jane Austen's day, "principles" and "morals" and "duty" were the words used to describe this sense of commitment to the standards that God has set for us in the Bible. Respect, honesty, humility, patience, self-control, modesty, loyalty, perseverance—these are the healthy guidelines for romance, the lines we are not to cross (as Marianne Dashwood learns the hard way). These are our inner principles.

Righteousness, then, is the outward behavior

toward others that comes from the inner principles or morals that we've adopted as our way of life. That's what righteousness means, in essence: *right relationships* with God and others (back to the two greatest commandments again).

Now of course the argument could be made that neither Darcy nor Elizabeth expresses any kind of outward faith in Jesus—not as we may think about it. We don't see them praying or going to church or talking about God (though Darcy does sign his letter to Lizzy with a poignant "God bless you"). But underlying the characters of Lizzy and Darcy are deeply held moral convictions that are expressed through righteous actions.

Let's start with Lizzy. Generally speaking, she chooses the wisest, most prudent approach to situations she faces, though she's also willing to acknowledge when she's messed up. With godly humility, she recognizes her own faults and feels genuine shame when she realizes she's been wrong. She's also honest; she speaks exactly what she thinks, and when she feels the lack of freedom to do so, she wisely says nothing (see James 1:26). Among other things, Lizzy doesn't degrade herself in order to win a mate; and she loves and tries to respect her parents, as the Bible asks us to do. As she changes and grows, her words and actions reflect a godlier attitude in all of these areas.

As for Darcy, despite his initial prickliness, he is a man of honesty and integrity who values speaking and acting upon the truth. "Disguise of every sort is my abhorrence," he tells Lizzy, and we realize the value of his honest qualities as the story progresses. We recognize that his character is consistent on the inside—he remains the same "in essentials"—even if his outward behavior changes from the beginning to the end of the story. Among other things, he pursues righteous actions out of love and concern for people and even takes care of the poor (see James 1:27). He knows when he's been wrong and works to make things right again. He, too, is able to mature and grow because he's willing to learn from his mistakes and do better next time.

Darcy's letter to Elizabeth is her first clue that there's more to this guy than meets the eye. She realizes, looking back, that she has never seen him do anything "unprincipled or unjust," nothing that goes against the teachings we find in the Bible (other than being proud and occasionally persnickety). It's an important moment in her understanding of Darcy's true character. But, as she soon discovers, his moral uprightness goes beyond the call of duty: Darcy treats the sin of others as an opportunity to act for the greater good of those involved, if at all possible. If he can't fix the situation, he can certainly do his best to make it better.

> ○ ⊜ ○
>
> She tried to recollect some instance of goodness, some distinguished trait of integrity or benevolence, that might rescue [Wickham] from the attacks of Mr. Darcy. . . . But no such recollection befriended her.
>
> LIZZY, REFLECTING ON WICKHAM'S OVERALL CHARACTER AFTER READING DARCY'S LETTER

Lizzy also realizes that, by contrast, there's been nothing especially virtuous about Wickham's behavior, though "his countenance, voice, and manner, had established him at once in the possession of every virtue." (Oh, how easily we fall into the same trap: judging a book by its cover, so to speak!) In his letter, Darcy makes the case that Wickham—for all of his deceptive appearances—actually has no inner moral principles whatsoever. It doesn't take long before we learn just how right Darcy is.

In that same letter, Darcy goes on to make what could be considered one of the most important statements about faith to be found in *Pride and Prejudice*. He says, "I knew that Mr. Wickham ought not to be a clergyman." In other words, the Church of England at the time might have ordained all sorts of weirdos like Mr. Collins, but that didn't make it right to put someone like Wickham in the pulpit. If a person who claims to be a Christian isn't walking the talk, and doesn't care how many people he hurts by his self-seeking behavior, then God's love is misrepresented to the world. This is true for *all* of us who claim to be Christians, too, not just Christian leaders. Jane Austen, through Darcy's comment, is making a powerful statement: We are not to be

Christians in name only, but followers of Jesus every moment, even when no one else is looking.

So what about your prospective Darcy (or Wickham)? What kind of faith is expressed in his outward behavior, even when you're not looking? If you were to ask him to write down the top ten priorities in his life, what would be on the list? How aware is he of his own faults and weaknesses? When was the last time he asked your forgiveness? Can you honestly say you know what he believes about God?

> How little of permanent happiness could belong to a couple who were only brought together because their passions were stronger than their virtue, she could easily conjecture.
>
> LIZZY, CONSIDERING LYDIA AND WICKHAM'S RELATIONSHIP

Grace

HOW TO GAUGE YOUR PEMBERLEY POTENTIAL

Above all, above respect and esteem, there was a motive within [Elizabeth] of good will [toward Darcy] which could not be overlooked. It was gratitude.—Gratitude, not merely for having once loved her, but for loving her still well enough, to forgive all the petulance and acrimony of her

> *manner in rejecting him, and all the unjust*
> *accusations accompanying her rejection.*
> *Pride and Prejudice*, VOLUME THREE, CHAPTER TWO

Okay, so let's say you've discussed all these faith issues. And let's say you've found the most awesome guy—a committed Christian who lives what he believes, who has the most DP of anyone you've met. If so, that's great! You could be headed down the road to a joyful, meaningful Pemberley together. But one word of caution (shades of Mary Bennet again): Don't assume just because a guy is a Christian that he's Mr. Perfect and will never mess up. Every guy will fail you—and you will fail him. That's just part of being human. And because failure is a given, one of the most important aspects of your relationship together is the spiritual principle of *grace*.

As Jane Austen well knew, moralizing on principles and duty is not an appropriate response to the longings and frustrations of the human heart. Yes, God has laid down rules for human relationships, born out of his great love for us and out of his plan for our lives. But this doesn't keep us from experiencing the heights of giddiness or the depths of sorrow. Loving others is messy business, as Darcy discovers, and sometimes the only thing that pulls everything together is grace.

While we may not know much about Darcy's personal relationship with God, his life can be seen as a parable of God's gracious relationship with us. Darcy exemplifies the biblical notion of grace—the free, undeserved gift that is given at great expense to the giver. He loves even when the object of his love has become as prickly and unlovable as possible. Not only that, but he goes out of his way to repair the relationship, sacrificing a great deal of time and money to restore what's left of Lydia's reputation so that Elizabeth and her family will not suffer disgrace. And along the way, he is willing to overlook the personal insults and injuries he has received from Wickham, going so far as to actually pay the man's debts.

No wonder Elizabeth feels gratitude toward

"Let me thank you again and again, in the name of all my family, for that generous compassion which induced you to take so much trouble, and bear so many mortifications, for the sake of discovering [Lydia and Wickham]."

LIZZY TO DARCY

him! He loves her still, even after all the awful things she has said, even after her coldness of manner and poor judgment. Darcy eventually wins Elizabeth over in the end, not because he "improves on acquaintance," but because of his self-sacrificing actions on behalf of her family. He goes beyond mere assistance, demonstrating a Christlike love that wonderfully parallels the lengths God goes to (and has gone to) to woo us as a beloved bride.

The ancient Greeks had a word for this kind of love: They called it *agape*, which pops up in the earliest Greek manuscripts of the Bible in places like 1 Corinthians 13. While we in the English-speaking world use one word, *love*, to describe all kinds of different experiences—from kissing a boyfriend to hugging a cat, calling our grandma, and choosing a flavor of Ben & Jerry's—the ancients had a different word for each of those things. Particularly, they focused on four kinds of love: romantic attraction (*eros*); affection (*storge*); friendship (*philia*); and a self-sacrificial, undeserved gift (*agape*).[9] And, now that you mention it, this entire book has focused on those four kinds of love, too, in terms of our dating relationships, family affections, friendships, and faith. (Wait a minute . . . was this on purpose?) So the Greeks were onto something.

But before you begin wondering what this has to do with Darcy, here's a curious thing: The word *agape*, when translated into the English Bible[10] of Jane Austen's day, becomes *charity*. Not the way we usually think about the word—as a nonprofit fund-raiser to help poor people—but as a gift of grace, a gesture of goodwill (and no, this has nothing to do with secondhand stores, either). Lizzy begins to feel "a motive . . . of good will" toward Darcy when she comprehends the depth of his love for her, and then later she tells Darcy that the last line of his letter was "charity itself." Darcy has made the shift from *eros* to *agape* love, and Lizzy recognizes the difference. What a contrast between Darcy's first proposal of marriage and his second! While his first attempt to win Lizzy's heart is abrupt, arrogant, and entirely focused on himself, his second wooing shows a humble awareness of all the factors in his life and hers. He puts *her* needs and the needs of others first, before his own. He pursues her gently and lovingly the second time around, taking into account both her family and his. If the first proposal failed in part because it wasn't delivered in "a more gentleman like manner," he is determined to be the gentleman this time.

Interestingly enough, the Holy Spirit has been described like a "gentleman" too, meaning that God treats us with courtesy and respect, despite the fact that he could easily overwhelm us by his power and presence. He doesn't force us to love him but waits patiently for us to open our hearts to him. Now, it's also true that at other times the Holy Spirit has been called "the Hound of Heaven"[11] (!), and certainly sometimes we feel like God is chasing us down. But it's a romantic pursuit in the spiritual sense. The

Hound of Heaven isn't an attack dog, but a rescue hound sent to save us when we're lost. That's the kind of pursuit Darcy is engaged in as he woos Elizabeth the second time; he literally becomes a rescuer for her and her family.

And far from rejecting him this time around, Lizzy opens her heart to a guy so deserving of her love. Once she realizes what he has done for her and her family, her natural response is gratitude.

> ● ⊕ ●
>
> Such a change in a man of so much pride, excited not only astonishment but gratitude—for to love, ardent love, it must be attributed.
>
> FROM *PRIDE AND PREJUDICE*

Grace and gratitude are important foundations to our own dating relationships. We need to recognize that our own Mr. Darcy is a gift we haven't earned or even deserved. God brings Mr. Darcys into our lives in part to help us grow into the women God has designed us to be from the beginning. And the proper response is gratitude, both to God and to Mr. Darcy. We must never take such love for granted.

God has brought you and your Mr. Darcy

together for a reason, and this is not an opportunity to be squandered by foolish and selfish behavior. (It *is* awfully difficult not to sound like preachy, condescending Mary Bennet! Perhaps if we substitute Elinor Dashwood from *Sense and Sensibility* instead, the cautionary comments might be a little easier to swallow.) This doesn't mean you have to talk about faith constantly when you're with your Mr. Darcy, but it *does* mean you invite God to be part of your dating relationship.

So what does this invitation look like? How do you integrate faith into your romance? Are we talking about going to church together and following a list of don'ts when it comes to intimacy? Well, yes, but that's only the beginning. Certainly at some point in your relationship you need to discuss issues about belief and doubt, spend time in prayer, and seek out Christian friends who can encourage both of you in your faith. And when you begin to talk seriously about becoming partners for life, it will be important to go to a pastor you know and trust to counsel you about Christian marriage.

But even these suggestions only barely touch the surface of why God might be drawing the two of you together.

Think of it in terms of Lizzy and Darcy for a moment. Remember how Lizzy marvels at the power Darcy has as master of Pemberley? "How many people's happiness [were] in his guardianship!—How much of pleasure or pain it was in his power to bestow!—How much of good or evil must be done by him!" She recognizes that he could make life miserable for a lot of people, but instead he chooses to love and serve them—including (and not least of all) the poor. Unlike Wickham, who will likely be a burden to the rest of the world for as long as he lives, Darcy has chosen to be a blessing.

And so has Lizzy. She has been the one, along with Jane, to keep a helpful attitude in the family, to take care of her parents, and to preserve the respectability of the Bennets in the eyes of the community. While both Lydia and Mrs. Bennet become burdens with their selfish behavior, Lizzy

seeks to lighten the load by offering laughter and a
sane perspective.

So imagine what Lizzy and Darcy will do when
they team up in the world! The Wickhams will be a
burden to everyone they know (and to many they
don't), but the Darcys at Pemberley will be a blessing
to all whose lives they touch. It's a pattern both Darcy
and Lizzy began long before they met and, we can
assume, will be their way of life together from this
point on.

When It's All Said and Done

For Christians, the call to a faith-filled romance
isn't just about acknowledging God's presence, but
about actively serving others together. How about you
and your Mr. Darcy? How will you bless others by
your relationship? You may want to start by creating
a mission statement as a couple. When the two of you
look around at a needy world, what are you most
passionate about? How will your relationship further

the work of God and bring justice to the world? That's your true Pemberley Potential. That's how you can be a blessing rather than a burden.

But, like Lizzy, your decision to be a blessing starts *now*, perhaps before Mr. Darcy comes along.

Part Five
THE ART OF REFLECTION

"Till this moment, I never knew myself."

ELIZABETH BENNET, VOLUME TWO, CHAPTER THIRTEEN

It happens to the best of us. You're going along one
day, minding your own business, when suddenly
you're struck by an idea that is utterly life-transform-
ing. We're not talking about a brilliant cure for cancer
or a definitive answer to whether or not Adam and Eve
had belly buttons. We're talking about a crucial
insight into something about yourself that you never
realized before.

One minute you're perfectly assured about your
life, confident about your personal goals and motiva-
tions, and the next minute, wham! You're standing
frozen in the middle of aisle six with an armload of
ramen noodles, blinking back tears.

Up to this point, you hadn't taken time to ask
yourself some tough questions regarding things
you've been most confident about: *What do I really want
in my life? Who have I become? Who do I want to be? Who do I
want to be with? And how well do I know the people I'm close to?
How well do they know me?* You now realize this lack of
self-knowledge is your own fault: You haven't bothered to take enough time alone for honest introspection. Perhaps part of this is because you don't like
being alone if you can help it. Friends provide the
perfect distraction, and maybe you prefer to keep the
conversation nice and fluffy. Even when you *are*
alone, you surround yourself with the shallow
virtual-communities of the TV or the Internet so
your mind doesn't wander into the deeper waters of
genuine self-analysis. But whatever the case, you're

inevitably alone at some point or another, and that's exactly when your mind betrays you.

All it takes is a few flashbacks of things you said or did—along with the sudden, painful memory of how people reacted to those things—and all your confidence comes crashing down at once. *Where* did you *ever* get the idea that you had such brilliant knowledge and insight to know the right thing to say or do in a given situation? The questions start piling higher and higher, deeper and deeper, till you feel buried under shame and remorse. Where your mind takes you, your conscience is sure to follow.

Well, sister, take heart. You're part of a noble tradition that includes all of the world's greatest heroines and heroes, including every last one of Jane Austen's leading characters. *Pride and Prejudice* has been called a "drama of self-discovery,"[12] and it's not hard to see why. Though we find Darcy's and Elizabeth's faults

> ☻ ☻ ☻
>
> Oh! how heartily did she grieve over every ungracious sensation she had ever encouraged, every saucy speech she had ever directed towards him.
>
> ELIZABETH, THINKING OF DARCY

endearing, we recognize how crucial it is that they discover the not-so-virtuous truth about themselves. Each goes through a time in which they reflect on what their prejudicial attitudes and behaviors have been. And this is precisely what makes them the stars of one of the greatest love stories of all time.

The turning point, of course, is Darcy's letter. For Darcy, the first assault of self-knowledge comes during Lizzy's rejection of his proposal, particularly with her famous words, "The mode of your declaration . . . spared me the concern which I might have felt in refusing you, had you behaved in a more gentleman like manner." Ouch! Then, as he writes the letter, Darcy begins a long process of introspection, tackling every one of his own motives, assumptions, attitudes, words, and actions. During the months following Lizzy's rejection, he eventually comes to see how very wrong he's been, even in regard to Bingley and Jane.

For Lizzy, the path to self-knowledge begins as she reads Darcy's words about Wickham. After several hours reflecting on Darcy's late-night scribblings, Lizzy finally recognizes that Wickham is badly flawed, despite his charms, while Darcy all along has only been doing his best to take care of the people he loves. She has been horribly wrong in her judgments of both men. And wrong about herself.

Jane Austen's heroes and heroines demonstrate just how very important the process of private reflection is to our own maturity, particularly in the arena of romantic love. If the dating game forms vital relational habits in us that we eventually bring into marriage, then probably the most important habit to develop is this one. If you're never alone—completely by yourself—in order to take a step back, to think about your relationships, to analyze your motives and the motives of others, and to be honest with yourself, then it's very easy to head down a path of willful self-deception that sets you up for getting hurt and for hurting everyone else.

For Jane Austen, the process of self-awareness wasn't just an interesting plot device to keep us on the edge of our seats till the final pages of her literary masterpieces. It was a profound spiritual truth that was at the heart of who she was as a person of faith.

This is obvious when we read the formal prayers she composed for those times of evening devotions when leadership of the household fell to her. There are only three of her prayers still in existence today, and their language and structure strongly echo what you would have heard during church worship services in nineteenth-century England. If you pick up an old copy of *The Book of Common Prayer*—the handbook for worship used by most congregations and Christian households in England at the time (and still used in the Church of England today)—you'll see a lot of similarities between that style of writing and Jane's prayers. So at first glance, her prayers don't seem all that significant.

But if you read closely, there's a recurring theme that is recognizable as uniquely Jane Austen, and that's the "insistence on self-knowledge."[13] Surprised? Nope! When we consider Jane's novels,

it's perfectly natural that her prayers echo some of
the things Elizabeth Bennet and Emma Woodhouse
and Marianne Dashwood express when they finally
discover the truth about themselves.

Certainly *The Book of Common Prayer* deals heavily
with our need to review and confess our sins before
God. But Jane Austen takes confession one step
further, insisting that we can't wait till we're sitting
in church before we take ourselves to task "for the
things we have done and the things we have left
undone." We need to be about the business of
self-knowledge on a daily, if not hourly, basis. The
health of our relationships with family, friends, and
God is at stake.

As Lizzy Bennet learns the hard way, one of our
human frailties is that we are finite in our perspective. We can see things only from our limited, often
self-seeking point of view. Faith helps us see
ourselves and others the way God sees us, to take a
higher, holier, broader view. God's perspective is
unerring and thorough; there is no deep part of our

souls that he does not see. And his perspective is colored by a profound and eternal love for us as we are. If we seek and apply God's perspective to what we think about ourselves and our darling Mr. Darcy, the truth comes into focus and we can finally see all our relationships clearly again.

But the art of reflection is similar to any other kind of art. Like watercolor or pottery, it takes time, practice, and persistence. We aren't necessarily good at it on the first try. And, like regular exercise, it's not always easy to get started in the first place. So, short of receiving a lengthy letter from our very own Mr. Darcy to force us into it, how do we go about the process on our own?

In the sections that follow, we'll consider some of the steps to aid in the practice of self-discovery. You'll notice that the process of reflection rather naturally follows a certain flow: from solitude to self-analysis, from self-analysis to confession, and from confession to moving forward. In fact, it's not hard to see how this echoes the character development of Jane Austen's leading ladies and gents. Hopefully it can aid in our own character development too.

Solitude

WHY YOU AND LIZZY BOTH CRAVE ALONE TIME

> *Reflection must be reserved for solitary hours; whenever she was alone, she gave way to it as the greatest relief; and not a day went by without a solitary walk, in which she might indulge in all the delight of unpleasant recollections.*
> *Pride and Prejudice*, VOLUME TWO, CHAPTER FOURTEEN

In the Bennet household, time to oneself is a precious commodity, particularly since the self-obsessed chatter of Mrs. Bennet, Lydia, and Kitty ensure that there's never a bit of quiet from one minute to the next. This explains why Mr. Bennet regularly retreats to his study and why Lizzy escapes to her room or to the outdoors and takes every opportunity to travel that she can. For Lizzy, the process of reflection is vital to keeping her sanity, and solitude is the key.

After wandering along the lane for two hours, giving way to every variety of thought; re-considering events, determining probabilities, and reconciling herself as well as she could, to a change so sudden and so important, fatigue, and a recollection of her long absence, made her at length return home; and she entered the house with the wish of appearing cheerful as usual, and the resolution of repressing such reflections as must make her unfit for conversation.

FROM *PRIDE AND PREJUDICE*

It's easy to see how Lizzy's quest for solitude is perhaps an echo of Jane Austen's own feelings on the subject. Remember: Jane grew up in a household of eight children and spent the bulk of her adult life surrounded by the social distractions of family, friends, and neighbors. In order to complete some of her novels, she escaped to her brother's house in London where she could spend quiet, uninterrupted hours alone. Solitude was no easy task in the intense domestic communities of Jane's day.

It's no easy task for us today, either, especially when friends, family, or classmates dominate every waking minute. Even when we're alone, we're surrounded by the continuous noise of talk radio, prime-time TV, i-Tunes, or the latest Norah Jones album (okay, so *some* things are worth listening to). But solitude is more than just being alone; it's being alone *in silence* so we can really concentrate on what God and our hearts are telling us. Solitude allows us time and space for self-analysis.

Where can you go to be by yourself? How can you schedule alone time for the purpose of honestly assessing your relationships? Long walks outside are one way Lizzy finds solitude. Mr. Bennet disappears into his study and shuts the door. Darcy already lives in a kind of grand solitude at Pemberley, a fact that probably accentuates his sense of loneliness without someone like Lizzy to keep him company. But he isn't the kind of guy to waste the hours in mindless activity; he uses the solitude to reflect on his behavior and improve his character, especially where Elizabeth Bennet is concerned.

Now, of course there's an inherent danger in too much solitude (that some of us can't avoid, if we live alone): If you don't return to society sooner or later, you can go off on emotional and psychological tangents that aren't particularly healthy. You can start obsessing about things that aren't nearly as important as you think and get all hung up about stupid stuff. One way to avoid this danger is to set yourself a cutting-off point, when you'll call a friend to go out for a latte.

But alone time comes first.

Self-Analysis

"HOW DESPICABLY I'VE ACTED!"

> *She grew absolutely ashamed of herself.—Of neither Darcy nor Wickham could she think, without feeling that she had been blind, partial, prejudiced, absurd.*
>
> *Pride and Prejudice*, VOLUME TWO, CHAPTER THIRTEEN

Darcy's letter is the point where the title of the story really should change from *Pride and Prejudice* to *Will and Grace*. Okay, maybe not. But you get the point. Reading Darcy's letter is what starts Lizzy on the upward climb toward self-knowledge. That's when she's forced to be honest with herself about pretty much everything.

"How despicably have I acted! . . . I, who have prided myself on my discernment!—I, who have valued myself on my abilities! who have often disdained the generous candour of my sister, and gratified my vanity, in useless or blameable distrust.— How humiliating is this discovery!—Yet, how just a humiliation!—Had I been in love, I could not have been more wretchedly blind. But vanity, not love, has been my folly.—Pleased with the preference of one, and offended by the neglect of the other, on the very beginning of our acquaintance, I have courted prepossession and ignorance, and driven reason away, where either were concerned. Till this moment, I never knew myself."

Ouch. No wonder all but the last line is cut from most film versions of the story! It's hard to keep Lizzy up there among our Top Ten Favorite Heroines when we hear this guilt-ridden grocery list of sins. We're tempted to say, "Oh, come *on*. You haven't been all *that* bad. It's not like you kissed Wickham or anything." But considering she's just unfairly insulted the nicest—and hottest—guy on the planet (not to mention turned down the opportunity to be his wife), her self-analysis is pretty fair.

The Bible asserts that wrongdoing is part of the spiritual DNA of every human being, including each one of us: "For everyone has sinned; we all fall short of God's glorious standard" (Romans 3:23). It's one of the basic beliefs of the Christian faith, as Jane Austen knew well. When describing a visit from her niece Anna, she writes in one of her letters, "It was quite a pleasure to see her, so young and so blooming, and so innocent, as if she had never had a wicked Thought in her Life, which yet one has some reason to suppose she must have had, if we believe the Doctrine of Original Sin,[14] or if we remember the events of her girlish days."[15] Ha! Another Austenian zinger.

If we take that understanding of original sin seriously, it means we must admit that none of us are exempt from saying or doing things that fall short of what God expects of us. You, too, have hurt the ones you love. The question is, how willing are you to admit it? What does it take for you to be honest with yourself?

> ⊖ ⊜ ⊖
> "I came to you without a doubt of my reception. You shewed me how insufficient were all my pretensions to please a woman worthy of being pleased."
> DARCY TO LIZZY

What Lizzy doesn't realize at first is that Darcy is also on the path of humility and honesty, which means they'll meet up again at some point, this time aware of their own weaknesses. Not a bad way to start life together, frankly. It can only go up from there.

Confession

GETTING IT ALL OUT IN THE OPEN

> *"I made a confession to [Bingley], which I believe I ought to have made long ago. I told him of all that had occurred to make my former interference in his affairs [with Jane], absurd and impertinent. . . . He has heartily forgiven me now."*
>
> MR. DARCY TO ELIZABETH, VOLUME THREE, CHAPTER SIXTEEN

Confession is the long-lost art of being honest with God and with others about the ways you've messed up. Perhaps that's why it's a lost art: Nobody wants to admit they make mistakes. But Jane Austen was highly aware of the importance of confession to our spiritual health and to the health of our relationships with family, friends, and romantic interests. This is obvious in her written prayers, but it also plays a large role in Lizzy and Darcy's ultimate reconciliation.

Darcy is the first to make a move towards an apology through his letter to Elizabeth, though he's too angry to manage more than a series of arguments in his own defense. First he justifies his behavior toward Wickham; but then he admits to being uneasy about his treatment of Bingley: "There is but one part of my conduct in the whole affair, on which I do not reflect with satisfaction; it is that I condescended to adopt the measures of art so far as to conceal from him your sister's being in town." This sounds promising by way of an "I'm

"What did you say of me, that I did not deserve? For, though your accusations were ill-founded, formed on mistaken premises, my behaviour to you at the time, had merited the severest reproof. It was unpardonable. I cannot think of it without abhorrence."

"We will not quarrel for the greater share of blame annexed to that evening," said Elizabeth; "The conduct of neither, if strictly examined, will be irreproachable."

DARCY AND LIZZY

sorry," but then he goes on to say, "It was done for the best.—On this subject I have nothing more to say, no other apology to offer." So much for confession!

But his attempt at explaining his behavior sets Lizzy thinking of the things *she* said and did during his marriage proposal that she now realizes were wrong. The problem is, while Darcy is able to write *her* something of an apology, Lizzy doesn't have the same freedom. For an unmarried young woman to write to a bachelor who isn't a member of her family would have been highly improper, according to the social rules of the time. (Imagine the same thing today! Good-bye, online chat . . .)

So Lizzy has to bottle it all up inside until she can share everything with Jane—all except the parts about Bingley, of course. Even though Darcy is the one who deserves Lizzy's apology, Lizzy knows it's better to tell *someone* than to pretend to the world that she's a perfect saint who never does anything wrong. The act of confession is important to keep a healthy perspective on her true character.

It's a lesson we can take to heart. After all, there's no point in being honest with yourself about the way you've treated others if you only go on pretending to the rest of the world that you were perfectly right in what you said or did. First comes the heartfelt apology to God for failing to be the person he created you to be—and you have God's assurance from the Bible that you are forgiven in Christ: "If we confess our sins to him, he is faithful and just to forgive us our sins and to cleanse us from all wickedness" (1 John 1:9). The second step is an apology to the person or people you've hurt. Here it gets a bit sticky. We all have a hard time forgiving and forgetting the sins of each other, as you've no doubt noticed when you've tried to forgive someone for something they've done to you. And yet it must be done.

The problem is, when it comes time to ask for forgiveness, we don't *like* admitting we've been wrong. It feels icky. We want people to think we're simply wonderful, that we never make mistakes, that we have it together all the time. Our "insufferable" pride takes over, and we try to justify everything we've done or said by providing every possible excuse we can. The stupid thing is that we're not fooling anyone. Everyone *else* knows we're not perfect. Our failure to admit our mistakes can hurt the ones we love even more than our imperfections do.

So what about you? To whom do you owe an apology lately? What will it take for you to admit you were wrong?

Moving Forward

THE NEXT STEP AFTER SELF-OBSESSED NAVEL-GAZING

> *Elizabeth's mind was now relieved from a very heavy weight; and, after half an hour's quiet reflection in her own room, she was able to join the others with tolerable composure.*
> *Pride and Prejudice*, VOLUME THREE, CHAPTER SEVENTEEN

Lizzy knows she's been wrong about Wickham and Darcy. But she doesn't try to gloss it over or cover it up. She doesn't make dumb excuses for herself. She confesses the truth to Jane, and eventually to Darcy, and moves forward with conviction.

Conviction is when we act on a belief. If we believe we have behaved badly, then we feel *convicted* to do something about it. We don't just bury ourselves in a sense of shame and despair. We move forward by attempting to right the wrong we have done and to do better next time. Through conviction we make the transition from reflection into meaningful action.

This is more than just about feeling sorry: It's about *repenting*. The word *repent* has an old-fashioned, biblical ring to it, but it was originally a traveling term, meaning basically, to make a U-turn. Repentance means you suddenly realize you've chosen the wrong road or path and now you must turn around and go back. It means having the humility to retrace your steps to the place where you got off track.

Lizzy is self-aware enough to

> ● ● ●
>
> When she remembered the style of his address, she was still full of indignation; but when she considered how unjustly she had condemned and upbraided him, her anger was turned against herself; and his disappointed feelings became the object of compassion.
>
> Lizzy, reflecting on Darcy's letter and first proposal

know she can't keep moving forward with the same attitudes and assumptions she's been operating under—not once she knows the truth about both Wickham and Darcy and comes to terms with her own lack of good judgment. She can't keep operating in the same way from now on. She must take a completely different path: She must turn around and start over again. One author has said, "Jane Austen's particular concern was to show that it is true knowledge of ourselves that makes us aware of our obligation to others and conditions our manner of dealing with them."[16] In other words, once we have a good handle on who we really are, our treatment of our friends and loved ones changes for the better.

As both Lizzy and Darcy demonstrate, you can't wallow in your sins. You can't forever see yourself as unforgivable and unlovable, lowering your own sense of self-esteem. Here we can't help but think of Georgiana Darcy. Lizzy surmises that Miss Darcy is shy in part because her self-esteem is so poor after what she did with Wickham. It will take her a long time to move on from feeling so ashamed, but Lizzy and Darcy will help by not treating her like a loser. She is forgiven. She's not doomed to make the same mistakes over and over again. And neither are you.

Your Christian faith assures you that you are loved and valued, no matter what you've done with Wickham.

> ◉ ◉ ◉
> This was a lucky recollection—it saved her from something like regret.
> FROM *PRIDE AND PREJUDICE*

Lizzy, too, experiences shame for misjudging both Wickham and Darcy, but she feels even worse about the things she *said* to Darcy in that regard. She would give anything to be able to apologize when she sees him next at Pemberley. But here Elizabeth is bound by her own dignity to wait for Darcy's move. She can't speak openly with him without looking like she's begging for a second proposal, so she must wait for him to speak first. But even so, she *is* taking action in a way, and that's in exercising good judgment. It may feel like she's powerless, but she certainly has it within her power to act foolishly, which she refuses to do. So she refrains from acting. She will not be desperate.

Today, we girls have much more freedom to act than in Jane Austen's time. We aren't bound by the constraints of society from approaching our friends, family, or even our boyfriends with an apology. But we do have to exercise good judgment in gauging the time and occasion. And we can't drag the confession out to an embarrassing degree or go on and on with our apologies to the point of irritation. We must make our case and move on.

Funny how romance brings us to the point of self-discovery so much quicker than perhaps any other circumstance! In the end, that's what God brings romantic love into our lives for, guys and girls alike: to help us see ourselves in light of our various relationships and to fulfill the potential God sees in us—DP, EP, and PP included.

When It's All Said and Done

So now you've walked through some of the elements of reflection in preparation for your own dramatic scene of self-discovery. But here are some ideas for resources that you might want to take with you into your times of solitude so you're able to stay focused on what's really important. That way, when you finally meet up with your girlfriends at Starbucks to talk it all over, you'll actually have meaningful things to say instead of the usual babble (theoretically speaking).

Of course, the most important resource you can bring into your times of reflection is the Bible. The discussion of self-knowledge as Jane Austen under-stood it is meaningless without getting a good handle on some of the biblical passages that she would have known well. But *Dating Mr. Darcy* isn't meant to be a Bible study, nor is it a devotional to aid in the daily study of Scripture. There are plenty of other resources out there (areUthirsty.com is a great place to start).

In Jane Austen's day, spiritual reading, or selecting books that provide encouragement for one's faith, was a common practice. Her options were probably quite limited compared to ours, consisting mostly of collections of sermons and various little tracts. One such humble treatise, given to her on the occasion of her confirmation in the Church of England when she was in her teens, was entitled *A Companion to the Altar: Shewing the Nature and Necessity of a Sacramental Preparation in Order to Our Worthy Receiving of Holy Communion, to Which Are Added Prayers and Meditations*(!). [17]

No joke. And she read it too.

Like we said, her options were a bit limited. But there's practically no end to the resources for spiritual reading we have today, and most of them are a billion times more interesting. *And*, we can safely say, the titles are shorter.

> "To all this she must yet add something more substantial, in the improvement of her mind by extensive reading."
>
> DARCY, DISCUSSING THE IDEAL WOMAN

Another resource that Jane Austen would have had on hand, as we've already mentioned, is *The Book of Common Prayer*. This handy little devotional resource contains specific ways that our times of prayer and worship can be structured so our minds stay focused.

It offers suggested prayers for different circumstances in the journey of faith and helps us concentrate on key passages in the Bible that relate to those
circumstances. This and other devotional resources
aren't meant to take the place of our own personal
conversations with God, but they can be a great help
when we have a hard time concentrating or can't
seem to find the words to say what we mean.
Although God "knows exactly what you need even
before you ask him" (Matthew 6:8), sometimes
prayers that others have written can help us discover
longings, needs, or mistaken ideas we didn't even
know we had.

A couple of other resources are located in the
last section of this book. The first is a brief Guide to
Reflection that takes you through several stages of
self-analysis. Call it a mini spiritual retreat. Pick an
afternoon when you ditch the clique and go off by
yourself to work through the suggested questions,
readings, and prayers—including excerpts from Jane
Austen's prayers. During your time alone, what

amazing Lizzy-style revelations hit you between the eyes (in a good way, of course)?

The last resource is what I call "Lizzy Bennet's Diary"—space for your own thoughts and reflections on the different relationships in your life. It includes quizzes to help you rate the DP, EP, and PP of your current (or prospective) romance and gives you a slightly more sensible grip on things than you might get from, oh, say, Bridget Jones. Remember: This is a *smart* girl's guide to romance.

Closing Thoughts

Closing Thoughts

*"I admire all my three sons-in-law highly," said he.
"Wickham, perhaps, is my favourite; but I think
I shall like your husband quite as well as Jane's."*

MR. BENNET TO ELIZABETH, VOLUME THREE, CHAPTER SEVENTEEN

By the end of *Pride and Prejudice*, the Bennets have
managed to secure every eligible and ineligible bachelor in the area, with the exception of Mr. Collins—
to whom they're related anyway. So the Darcys and
Bingleys and Wickhams and Collinses and Bennets

are now all family, not to mention Lady Catherine de Bourgh. Can't you just picture Christmas dinner at Pemberley? And you thought your family reunions were a mess!

But somehow those crazy relationships seem insignificant next to the fabulous triumph of seeing Elizabeth Bennet and Fitzwilliam Darcy finally together. Somehow our delightful heroine and faithful hero have overcome their initial differences and are now able to create a life together that, rather than being an exclusive love nest, is a place where their vastly different friends and families are welcome and blessed.

They still have lots of work to do when it comes to getting along with everybody, however. Darcy has to learn how to endure Lizzy's mother (even the good-natured Bingleys move far away from Longbourn eventually, just so they don't

> "I am the happiest creature in the world. Perhaps other people have said so before, but not one with such justice. I am happier even than Jane; she only smiles, I laugh. Mr. Darcy sends you all the love in the world, that he can spare from me. You are all to come to Pemberley at Christmas."
>
> LIZZY, IN A LETTER TO HER AUNT

have to deal with Mrs. Bennet!), and Lizzy somehow has to face Lady Catherine again. The Darcys don't go so far as to ever welcome Wickham into their home—remember all that business about establishing healthy boundaries?—but that's understandable when you consider the effect it would have on Georgiana. There's work to do on all sides.

If you and your Mr. Darcy are currently an item, now is a good time to assess how well you're doing in terms of your interactions with each other's friends and family. How do you integrate your friends into your dating relationship, short of taking your favorite gal pal along as a chaperone (eek!)? Some ideas include spending time with his (and your) friends and family members one-on-one, asking questions, looking at photo albums, learning the history of the relationships, taking note of what they value, believe, like, and dislike, as well as how they communicate and handle conflict. Be creative.

Then, when it's time to look down the road toward a future together, consider if you can create a healthy Pemberley with this guy, the kind of romance that welcomes and invites your friends and family—as difficult as they might be at times—rather than shuts them out. When comparing the Darcys to the Wickhams, it's easy to see how the Darcys are the best equipped to fulfill God's ultimate goal for marriage, which is for us to be a blessing to the world rather than a burden.

Meanwhile, enjoy the wonderful adventure of dating Mr. Darcy!

Extra Stuff

A. GUIDE TO REFLECTION

Like the central plot of *Pride and Prejudice*, your life is a
"drama of self-discovery," one that is inevitably spiritual in its implications. You can't discover who you
really are unless you understand yourself as a sinful
yet beloved and forgiven human being. As we've
already said, your story is a divine romance in which
God is wooing you back to himself. It's also a divine
comedy, a story that ultimately has a happy ending if
you choose to accept God's grace and forgiveness in
Christ. But the plot devices of self-discovery, divine

romance, and happy ending are all impossible without the scene where the main character (you) reaches a point of self-awareness. What does it take before you finally say, "Till this moment, I never knew myself"?

The following is a guided tour through the soul for the purpose of private reflection. It follows the four-part pattern of solitude, self-analysis, confession, and moving forward, as discussed in part five. Each part includes quotes from the prayers of Jane Austen, probing questions, and suggested Bible readings (references in this book are to the New Living Translation), all for the purpose of helping you reflect on your internal character. How well do you really know yourself? How are you doing in your relationships with family, friends, and God? How willing are you to acknowledge when you've messed up? How will you move on from here into positive, healthy attitudes and actions?

Find a time and place to be alone (possibly in your room this evening?), and then dive in!

Solitude

From the prayers of Jane Austen:[18]

> *Another day is now gone, and added to those, for which we were before accountable. Teach us Almighty Father, to consider this solemn truth, as we should do, that we may feel the importance of every day, and every hour as it passes, and earnestly strive to make a better use of what Thy goodness may yet bestow on us, than we have done of the time past.*
>
> *Amen.*

QUESTIONS TO THINK ABOUT:

How difficult is it for me to be alone? Why?

How, when, and where will I intentionally seek solitude for the purpose of reflection?

What will I do when I'm alone? What tools can I bring with me to help in the process of reflection?

What topics will I consider?

Suggested readings: Psalm 46:10; Mark 1:35; Mark 6:30-32
My prayer:

Self-Analysis

From the prayers of Jane Austen:[19]

> *Teach us to understand the sinfulness of our own hearts, and
> bring to our knowledge every fault of temper and every evil habit
> in which we have indulged to the discomfort of our fellow-
> creatures, and the danger of our own souls. May we now, and on
> each return of night, consider how the past day has been spent by
> us, what have been our prevailing thoughts, words and actions
> during it, and how far we can acquit ourselves of evil. Have we
> thought irreverently of Thee, have we disobeyed Thy
> commandments, have we neglected any known duty, or willingly
> given pain to any human being? Incline us to ask our heart these
> questions oh! God, and save us from deceiving ourselves by pride
> or vanity.*
>
> *Amen.*

QUESTIONS TO THINK ABOUT:

What are my top five strengths?

What are my top five weaknesses?

What are my main goals in life? What am I doing to achieve those goals?

What do my goals show me about myself?

How do these goals affect my relationships with family, friends, and God?

In what ways have I sinned against my loved ones through the unkind things I've thought, said, or done? In what ways have I failed to do the kind things I know I should have?

How healthy are my relationships in general?

(Note: For this part, it may be helpful—and entertaining!—to spend a good hour or so working through the material in Lizzy Bennet's Diary found in the next section of this book. When you're through, come back and wrap up the rest of this guided reflection as outlined below.)

Suggested reading: Psalm 51:1-12
My prayer:

Confession

From the prayers of Jane Austen:[20]

Pardon oh! God the offences of the past day. We are conscious of many frailties; we remember with shame and contrition, many evil thoughts and neglected duties; and we have perhaps sinned against Thee and against our fellow-creatures in many instances of which we have no remembrances. Pardon oh God! whatever Thou has seen amiss in us, and give us a stronger desire of resisting every evil inclination and weakening every habit of sin. Thou knowest the infirmity of our nature, and the temptations which surround us. Be Thou merciful, oh heavenly Father! to creatures so formed and situated.

Incline us oh God! to think humbly of ourselves, to be severe only in the examination of our own conduct, to consider our fellow-creatures with kindness, and to judge of all they say and do with that charity which we would desire from them ourselves.

Amen.

Questions to think about:

To whom do I owe an apology lately? Why?

What will it take for me to admit I was wrong?

(Here's an idea: Make a list of all the possible excuses you could give for your behavior and then cross them out one by one. Write "I was wrong" at the end of the list—you may even want to circle it.)

If I can't yet confess to the person I've wronged, who else can I talk to?

What will it take for me to recognize that God forgives me and to accept his forgiveness?

Suggested reading: Psalm 32:1–5; James 5:16; 1 John 1:8–9
My prayer:

Moving Forward

From the prayers of Jane Austen:[21]

> *Look with mercy on the sins we have this day committed and in
> mercy make us feel them deeply, that our repentance may be
> sincere, & our resolutions stedfast of endeavoring against the
> commission of such in future.*
>
> *Give us grace to endeavor after a truly Christian spirit to
> seek to attain that temper of forbearance and patience of which
> our blessed Saviour has set us the highest example; and which,
> while it prepares us for the spiritual happiness of the life to come,
> will secure to us the best enjoyment of what this world can give.*
>
> *May the comforts of every day, be thankfully felt by us,
> may they prompt a willing obedience of Thy commandments and
> a benevolent spirit toward every fellow-creature.*
>
> *Amen.*

QUESTIONS TO THINK ABOUT:

What have I learned about myself?

How will this new knowledge about myself be obvious in
how I act? in my attitudes? thoughts? words?

What steps can I take to make things right in my relationships with family? with friends? with God?

Suggested reading: John 15:12; Ephesians 4:1–3; Philippians 4:13

My prayer:

B. LIZZY BENNET'S DIARY

Okay, so you're not nearly as self-obsessed as Bridget Jones (thank heaven!). But she's onto something when it comes to working out relational issues on paper. Here's your chance for literary expression. Give yourself an hour or two (or five minutes a day for the next week or so) and see if you can come to a better understanding of yourself and your Mr. Darcy through the medium of a personal diary. Below are some possible entries to get you started in regard to your relationships, followed by similar questions regarding Darcy and his world. When it's all said and done, what's your EP? What's his DP? And together what's your PP? (Oh, and if you also want to count your calories along the way, fine, but don't get too obsessed with what's happening on the outside. We're talking inner issues here.)

Feel free to write all over these pages. If there is no Darcy in your life right now, fill out his sections with your ideal date in mind.

Entry #1: My Family

MOM (STEPMOM, GUARDIAN, OTHER)

Name

Occupation

Personality (Is she like Mrs. Bennet, Mrs. Gardiner, Lady Catherine de Bourgh, some other Jane Austen character?)

Things that stress her out

Things that make her happy

Things we have in common/like to do together

Biggest unresolved issue(s) between us

    Quality of relationship with Mom on scale of 1 to 10 (1 being v. v. bad, 10 being v. v. good):

    when it comes to respect, as discussed in part two: ___

    when it comes to communication: ___

when it comes to integrity (being the same person with Mom as I am with friends, coworkers, etc.): ___
Total score divided by 3: ___

If flunking hopelessly with Mom, I am determined to

If getting along famously, I will thank her by

If somewhere in between, I will thank her and resolve to

DAD (STEPDAD, GUARDIAN, OTHER)
Name

Occupation

Personality (Is he like Mr. Bennet, Mr. Gardiner, Mr. Lucas, etc.?)

Things that stress him out

Things that make him happy

Things we have in common/like to do together

Biggest unresolved issue(s) between us

    Quality of relationship with Dad on scale of 1 to 10:
    when it comes to respect: ___
    communication: ___
    integrity: ___
    Total score divided by 3: ___

If flunking hopelessly with Dad, I am determined to

If getting along famously, I will thank him by

If somewhere in between, I will thank him and resolve to

OTHER KEY FAMILY MEMBERS TO NOTE

List, with observations, in similar manner to above:

Siblings/stepsiblings, etc.

Aunts, uncles, cousins, grandparents

Others

Quality of relationship with each of above on scale
of 1 to 10:
when it comes to respect: ____
communication: ____
integrity: ____
Total score divided by 3: ____

Ways I'm determined to improve above

> "Well, [Mr. Bingley]
> certainly is very
> agreeable, and I give
> you leave to like him.
> You have liked many
> a stupider person."
>
> LIZZY TO JANE

GENERAL OBSERVATIONS:
Things to celebrate about my loony,
lovable family

Things I can't stand about them

How many hours I spend with family each day/week/
month/year when not at school/coffeehouse/depressing
meeting

Ways I'm determined to improve quality time with family

Entry #2: Darcy's Family
HIS MOM (STEPMOM, GUARDIAN, OTHER)
Name

Occupation

Personality

Things that stress her out

Things that make her happy

Things Darcy and Mom have in common/like to do
together

Biggest unresolved issue(s) between them

    Quality of his relationship with Mom on scale
of I to IO:
    when it comes to respect: ____
    communication: ____
    integrity: ____
    Total score divided by 3: ____

My gut reaction to above (am delighted? mildly
concerned? running in opposite direction at full speed?)

Action items/things to discuss with Darcy about Mom
(if I dare)

HIS DAD (STEPDAD, GUARDIAN, OTHER)
Name

Occupation

Personality

Things that stress him out

Things that make him happy

Things Darcy and Dad have in common/like to do
together

Biggest unresolved issue(s) between them

Quality of Darcy's relationship with Dad on scale of
1 to 10:
   when it comes to respect: ___
   communication: ___
   integrity: ___
   Total score divided by 3: ___

My gut reaction to above (pleased?
mildly troubled? purchasing plane
ticket to Hong Kong?)

Action items/things to discuss with
Darcy about Dad (take deep breath)

DARCY'S OTHER KEY FAMILY
MEMBERS TO NOTE

List, with observations, in similar manner to above:
Siblings/stepsiblings, etc.

> ⊖ ☺ ⊖
>
> "May I ask to what
> these questions tend?"
> "Merely to the
> illustration of your
> character. . . . I am
> trying to make it out."
> "And what is your
> success?"
> She shook her head.
> "I do not get on at all.
> I hear such different
> accounts of you as
> puzzle me exceedingly."
>
> VERBAL SPARRING
> BETWEEN DARCY AND
> LIZZY

Aunts, uncles, cousins, grandparents

Others

    Quality of his relationship to each of above on scale of I to IO:

when it comes to respect: ____

communication: ____

integrity: ____

Total score divided by 3: ____

Action items/things to discuss with Darcy about family members

GENERAL OBSERVATIONS ABOUT DARCY'S FAMILY:

Things to celebrate about his loony, lovable family

Things he can't stand about them

How many hours he spends with family each day/week/
month/year when not at school/gym/depressing meeting

Ways I can encourage him to improve quality time with
family

Entry #3: Dealing with Each Other's Families

Quality of my relationship with Darcy's family on scale of 1 to 10:

when it comes to respect: ___

communication: ___

integrity: ___

Total score divided by 3: ___

Quality of Darcy's relationship with my family on scale of 1 to 10:

when it comes to respect: ___

communication: ___

integrity: ___

Total score divided by 3: ___

Can I be a good daughter or sibling when dating this guy, or do I feel pressured to squash or ignore that part of myself?

Hmm . . .

Entry #4: My Friends

Create separate lists for each of my friends as follows:

NAME:

Personality (Is she like Charlotte, Jane, Miss Bingley?)

Things that stress her out

Things that make her happy

Things we have in common/like to do together

Biggest unresolved issue(s) between us

> Quality of relationship on scale of 1 to 10:
> when it comes to communication, as discussed in
> part three: ___
> respect: ___
> loyalty: ___
> Total score divided by 3: ___

What does score indicate about friend (Is she a good, bad, mildly annoying, overall decent person to have in my life?)

What does score indicate about self (Blunt honesty here: capable of quality relationships? room for improvement?)

GENERAL OBSERVATIONS ABOUT FRIENDS:
Things to celebrate about loony, lovable friends

Things I can't stand about friends

How many hours I spend with friends when not at home/school/mall/depressing meeting (includes phone calls, e-mail, instant messaging, etc.)

Ways I'm determined to improve quality time with friends

"Poor Eliza!—to be only just tolerable."
CHARLOTTE LUCAS, MAKING A JOKE OUT OF DARCY'S WORDS ABOUT LIZZY

Entry #5: Darcy's Friends

Create separate lists for each of Darcy's friends as follows:

NAME:

Personality (Is Darcy's friend like Bingley, Colonel Fitzwilliam, Wickham?)

Things that stress him out

Things that make him happy

Things he and Darcy have in common/like to do together

Biggest unresolved issue(s) between them

Quality of relationship on scale of 1 to 10:
when it comes to communication: ____
respect: ____
loyalty: ____
Total score divided by 3: ____

What does score indicate about friend (Is he a good, bad, mildly annoying, overall decent person for Darcy to have in his life?)

What does score indicate about Darcy (Blunt honesty here: capable of quality relationships? room for improvement?)

GENERAL OBSERVATIONS ABOUT FRIENDS:
Things to celebrate about Darcy's loony, lovable friends

Things he can't stand about his friends

How many hours he spends with friends when not at home/school/lake house/depressing meeting (includes phone calls, e-mail, instant messenging, etc.)

Ways I can encourage him to improve quality time with friends

Entry #6: Dealing with Each Other's Friends

Quality of my relationship with Darcy's friends on scale of 1 to 10:

when it comes to respect: ___

communication: ___

loyalty: ___

Total score divided by 3: ___

Quality of Darcy's relationship with my friends on scale of 1 to 10:

when it comes to respect: ___

communication: ___

loyalty: ___

Total score divided by 3: ___

Can I be a good friend to others when I'm with this guy, or do I feel like I must squash or ignore that part of myself?

Hmm . . .

Entry #7: My Faith

Church background, if any

Questions I have about faith right now

Ways I'm trying to grow spiritually

Time spent doing faith-related things per week (prayer, Bible study, devotions, church, youth group, serving others, etc.)

Bad habits (attitudes, words, behavior) to get rid of

Good habits to develop

Quality of my relationship with God on scale of 1 to 10:

when it comes to accepting his forgiveness and grace: ___

when it comes to following through on what he wants me to do: ___

when it comes to being honest with others about my faith, not hiding my faith from them: ___

Total score divided by 3: ___

Entry #8: Darcy's Faith

Church background, if any

Questions Darcy has about faith right now

Ways he's trying to grow spiritually

Time he spends doing faith-related things per week
(prayer, Bible study, devotions, church, youth group,
serving others, etc.)

Bad habits (attitudes, words, behavior) he struggles with

Good habits he can develop

    Quality of his relationship with God on scale
of 1 to 10:
        when it comes to accepting God's forgiveness and
        grace: ___
        when it comes to following through on what God
        wants him to do: ___
        when it comes to being honest with others about his
        faith, not hiding his faith from them: ___
        Total score divided by 3: ___

Entry #9: Dealing with Each Other's Faith

Amount of time spent doing faith-related things together per week (discussing our questions and doubts, Bible study, prayer, church, serving others, etc.)

Ways we encourage each other to grow spiritually

Ways our relationship sometimes hinders each other's faith

Some things we need to work on

Quality of our interaction with each other's faith on scale of 1 to 10:

when it comes to making faith an important part of our relationship: ___

when it comes to humility and grace in our treatment of each other: ___

when it comes to being a blessing to the rest of the world: ___

Total score divided by 3: ___

Can I be an honest Christian with this guy, or do I feel like I have to squash or ignore that side of myself?

Hmm . . .

Entry #10: Conclusions
My EP (Elizabeth Potential)

Glance through final scores related to self in each section.

Which relationships have highest scores?

Which require most work?

What does that tell self about self?

On scale of 1 to 10 (1 being v. v. low, 10 being v. v. high), how high is my overall EP? __

    (If scored below 5, recommend Emergency Chick-Flick Marathon consisting of all Jane Austen films produced in last ten years, followed by complete Lizzy Makeover in retro-Regency ballroom-wear.)

His DP (Darcy Potential)

Glance through final scores related to Darcy in each section.

Which relationships have highest scores?

Which require most work?

What does that tell self about Darcy?

On scale of 1 to 10, how high is his overall DP? ___

(If scored below 5, recommend hiring consultant from Regency Eye for the Hip-Hop Guy, starting with belt for pants and quick lesson on bowing when in the presence of females.)

> ⊖ 😊 ⊖
>
> She began now to comprehend that he was exactly the man, who, in disposition and talents, would most suit her.
>
> LIZZY,
> THINKING OF DARCY

Our PP (Pemberley Potential)

Glance through final scores related to how self and Darcy interact with each other's relationships.

Which relationships have highest scores?

Which require most work?

What does that say about us together?

On scale of 1 to 10, how high is our overall PP? ___

    (If scored below 5, recommend fleeing to country estate in Derbyshire for two weeks, with chaperone, in order to educate on finer points of polite conversation, dancing a reel, and falling in love sensibly.)

Characters in
Pride and Prejudice

ELIZABETH BENNET, HER FAMILY, AND FRIENDS

Elizabeth Bennet The main heroine in the story; the second eldest and most sensible of the five Bennet sisters. Affectionately known as "Lizzy" or "Eliza" among her family and friends, she is intelligent, fun-loving, and pretty—though her independent spirit keeps her from needing the attentions of the opposite sex. She meets and misjudges the character of Mr. Darcy at the beginning; it takes the entire rest of the story to bring them together in the end.

Mr. Bennet Lizzy's smart, cynical, loving, yet ultimately negligent father. He married his wife, Mrs. Bennet, for her looks and has regretted it ever since.

Mrs. Bennet Lizzy's flighty, selfish mother whose primary motivation is to find rich husbands for her five daughters.

Jane Bennet Lizzy's sweet, gentle eldest sister and best friend; also referred to as "Miss Bennet." Jane falls in love with Mr. Darcy's friend Mr. Bingley from the beginning, but Darcy and Bingley's sisters contrive to keep him and Jane apart until the end of the story.

Mary Bennet The middle daughter of the five. She's the annoying, self-righteous know-it-all who prefers books to people but isn't nearly as smart as she thinks.

Catherine (Kitty) Bennet The second-youngest of Lizzy's sisters; almost as silly as her mother.

Lydia Bennet Lizzy's youngest sister and Mrs. Bennet's favorite. Because she's spoiled and her father does nothing to check her wild, flirtatious behavior, she manages—at the age of sixteen—to run off with the charming yet villainous Mr. Wickham. Her behavior ruins her reputation, as well as the reputation of her entire family, until Mr. Darcy steps in and makes Wickham marry her.

Mr. and Mrs. Gardiner Lizzy's caring, sensible uncle and aunt who are essentially surrogate parents for her and Jane. Because Mr. Gardiner is a businessman in London's Cheapside, an unfashionable part of town, Lizzy's relatives are initially sneered at by those in Darcy's circle. Eventually Darcy recognizes the sterling worth of the Gardiners and seeks them out when Lydia runs away.

Mr. Collins The pompous, ridiculous, and "odious" cousin of the Bennet sisters; heir to their father's house and property. He visits the family in order to marry one of the girls, selecting Lizzy at first, only to be rejected. He marries her good friend Charlotte Lucas instead.

Charlotte Lucas Lizzy's good friend who we think is fairly sensible until she makes the baffling decision to marry Mr. Collins. It's at Charlotte's new home that Lizzy receives her first offer of marriage from Mr. Darcy.

Maria Lucas The sister of Charlotte, who travels with Lizzy and Sir William (see below) to visit the newly married Collinses.

Sir William Lucas The sociable but rather pompous father of Charlotte.

Mr. Wickham A cute and charming young officer in the nearby regiment who initially wins the admiration of Lizzy, but proves himself villainous by running off with her sister. Wickham was raised in Darcy's household and is responsible for spreading the false rumors about Darcy at the beginning of the story. The truth is that Wickham misused Darcy by squandering his money and attempting to elope with Darcy's sister.

Colonel and Mrs. Forster The colonel of Wickham's regiment and his immature young wife. It is Mrs. Forster who invites Lydia to join her in Brighton.

MR. DARCY, HIS FAMILY, AND FRIENDS

Fitzwilliam Darcy The handsome, noble (and rich) hero of the story who undergoes a transformation of attitude from being proud and arrogant to humble and considerate. He has always been loving and generous to family and friends but fails to show that side of himself to Elizabeth Bennet until after she rejects his first proposal of marriage. Then he sacrifices his time, money, and pride to save her family from disgrace when Lydia runs off with Wickham, demonstrating both his change of heart and the depth of his love for Lizzy.

Charles Bingley Cute, friendly, and compliant, Bingley is Darcy's best friend. He falls in love with Jane Bennet at the beginning of the story and eventually marries her, despite the objections of his sisters.

Caroline Bingley Along with the arrogant Mrs. Hurst, Miss Bingley is Charles's snobby and self-centered sister. She is trying to win Mr. Darcy for herself, and thus despises Lizzy. She also pretends to befriend Jane at first but then helps Darcy keep Bingley and Jane apart.

Georgiana Darcy Darcy's only sibling, ten years younger than himself. She is shy and self-conscious, mostly because of her mishaps with Wickham, but welcomes Lizzy as a sister. It's in part because of Darcy's loving treatment of Miss Darcy that Lizzy begins to see the genuine kindness of his character.

Colonel Fitzwilliam Darcy's cousin who takes an interest in Lizzy while she visits Charlotte and Mr. Collins near the home of Darcy's aunt (see below). It's Colonel Fitzwilliam who unwittingly tells Lizzy of Darcy's successful attempt to keep Bingley and Jane apart.

Lady Catherine de Bourgh Darcy's rich, arrogant aunt, who also happens to be the condescending patroness whom Mr. Collins treats like royalty in his parish. When Lady Catherine hears the rumor that Darcy and Elizabeth will soon be engaged, she visits Lizzy personally to condemn the match, saying that Darcy is intended for Lady Catherine's own daughter, Miss de Bourgh, instead.

Miss de Bourgh Lady Catherine's pale, sickly daughter, the supposed fiancée of Mr. Darcy.

Locations in Pride and Prejudice

Brighton The large town to which Wickham's regiment is sent after their stay in Meryton. Lydia is unwisely allowed to go to Brighton as a companion to the wife of Colonel Forster and ends up running away to London with Wickham.

Derbyshire The "county" where Lizzy and the Gardiners travel on vacation; it's also the location of Pemberley. There Lizzy begins to see Darcy in a new light and eventually realizes she's in love with him.

Gracechurch-street, Cheapside The section of London where the Gardiners live. It's considered unfashionable by Darcy's inner circle but is perfectly respectable.

Hertfordshire The English "county" where the previous villages and estates are located.

Hunsford Parsonage The home of Charlotte and Mr. Collins in the region of Kent, near the estate of Darcy's aunt, Lady Catherine.

Lambton The little village in Derbyshire near Pemberley where Lizzy and the Gardiners stay on their tour.

Longbourn The tiny village where the Bennets make their home.

Lucas Lodge The home of Sir William and Lady Lucas, Charlotte, Maria, and siblings.

Meryton The nearest village to Longbourn. This is where the dance takes place when Lizzy and Darcy see each other for the first time, and this is where Wickham's regiment is stationed.

Netherfield House The estate near Meryton that Bingley rents. It's because of his residence there that he, his sisters, and Darcy meet the Bennets.

Rosings Park The vast and ostentatious estate of Lady Catherine de Bourgh.

Pemberley House The grand yet taste-ful estate of Mr. Darcy and his sister, located in Derbyshire.

Endnotes

1 Letter from Jane Austen to her sister, Cassandra, January 1813. Deirdre Le Faye, ed., *Jane Austen's Letters* (Oxford: Oxford University Press, 1995), 201.

2 From *The Book of Common Prayer*, 1979 edition, http://justus.anglican.org/resources/bcp/euchr1.pdf.

3 Le Faye, *Letters*, 332.

4 Ibid, 156–157.

5 Irene Collins, *Jane Austen and the Clergy* (London: Hambledon and London, 1994), 169.

6 Anglicans Online: The Catechism, http://anglicansonline.org/basics/catechism.html.

7 Collins, *Clergy*, 195.

8 Most of Jane Austen's works (all of which are in the public domain) are printed online at www.pemberley.com. This quote is found at http://www.pemberley.com/etext/SandS/chapter46.htm.

9 For a more in-depth discussion, see C. S. Lewis's classic book *The Four Loves*.

10 The King James Version.

11 A poem by Francis Thompson.

12 Bruce Stovel, "'A Nation Improving in Religion': Jane Austen's Prayers and Their Place in Her Life and Art," *Persuasions* (December 1994): 194.

[13] Ibid.

[14] From the Thirty-Nine Articles of Religion of the Church of England, number IX, http://anglicansonline.org/basics/thirty-nine_articles.html.

[15] Le Faye, *Letters*, 330.

[16] Collins, *Clergy*, 153.

[17] A companion volume to *The Book of Common Prayer*, written by William Vickers and published in various editions throughout the eighteenth century.

[18] From *The Minor Works of Jane Austen* (public domain).

[19] Ibid.

[20] Ibid.

[21] Ibid.

WALKING
THROUGH THE
WARDROBE

A devotional quest into
The Lion, the Witch and the Wardrobe

THE NEW BOOK BY
SARAH ARTHUR

COMING
OCTOBER 2005

ISBN 1-4143-0766-7

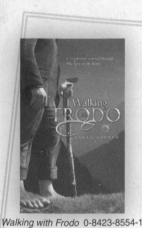
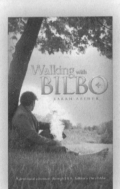

Compact

Metal

Bible

Any
Questions?

Available wherever Bibles are sold

areUthirsty.com

well . . . are you?